LESSONS OF THE LOTUS

BHANTE Y. WIMALA

LESSONS OF THE LOTUS

PRACTICAL SPIRITUAL TEACHINGS OF A TRAVELING BUDDHIST MONK

*Foreword by His Holiness
the Dalai Lama*

BANTAM BOOKS
NEW YORK TORONTO LONDON
SYDNEY AUCKLAND

LESSONS OF THE LOTUS

A Bantam Book/December 1997

BOOK DESIGN BY ELLEN CIPRIANO

Library of Congress Cataloging-in-Publication Data

Wimala, Bhante Y.

Lessons of the Lotus : practical spiritual teachings of a traveling Buddhist monk / Bhante Y. Wimala.

p.   cm.

ISBN 0-553-37855-4 (pbk.)

1. Religious life—Buddhism.   2. Buddhism—Doctrines.   I. Title.

BQ4302.W56   1997

294.3'4—dc21   97-13258

CIP

Published simultaneously in the United States and Canada

Bantam Books are published by Bantam Books, a division of Bantam Double-day Dell Publishing Group, Inc. Its trademark, consisting of the words "Bantam Books" and the portrayal of a rooster, is Registered in U.S. Patent and Trademark Office and in other countries. Marca Registrada. Bantam Books, 1540 Broadway, New York, New York 10036.

PRINTED IN THE UNITED STATES OF AMERICA

FFG   10 9 8 7 6 5 4 3 2 1

*With gratitude and respect I dedicate this
book to my teachers, whose love, wisdom,
and guidance inspired me to continue on
my spiritual path.*

*And to all my friends and students around
the world, who contribute so much to make
my travel and teaching possible.*

CONTENTS

LESSONS OF THE LOTUS

FOREWORD

Bhante Wimala is a Theravada Buddhist monk from Sri Lanka who spends his time traveling and teaching in the spirit of monks at the time of the Buddha. I am not surprised that many people are drawn to listen to him wherever he goes, because he presents the teachings the Buddha gave over 2,500 years ago as if they had been given to address the needs of people today. His counsel to those who meet him is drawn from his own experience and the inspiration he has gained from studying and contemplating the Buddha's teachings.

The topics he touches on in this book range widely, from the miracle of human life and ways to cultivate faith and self-esteem, to discussions of the relationship between bees and flowers. On a simple and practical level, he explains how meditation functions as a healing force for the mind. He emphasizes meditation on the breath, which, as he points out, is always available to calm your mind. In addition to these simple methods for dealing with our own inner problems, he also discusses global problems such as the pollution and degeneration of our environment.

Bhante Wimala's heartfelt concern for the suffering and the simple remedies he draws from the Buddha's teachings will be a source of strength for everyone confused by the pressures of modern life.

January 10, 1997

ACKNOWLEDGMENTS

I am deeply grateful to everyone who has contributed to the birthing of *Lessons of the Lotus*. My heartfelt thanks go to:

Brian Tart of Bantam Books, who invited me to write the book. His encouragement, advice, and guidance made it easier for me to continue writing.

My personal managing editor, Kingsley Rajapkse, for his dedication in nursing the project from the outset in the form of his warm personal attention to the project, his dependability, his cheerful assistance and patience, and his contribution in making a somewhat serious spiritual project an enjoyable experience.

Reverend K. Dhammavasa and Reverend Mudita for inviting me to stay at their temple in Mississauga, Canada, and allowing me to make the Mississauga temple my home while I was writing the manuscript. I am thankful to them for providing me with separate quarters in which I had privacy and peace and for taking care of all my needs. During my five-month stay in Canada we shared many stories, moments of laughter, and insightful dialogues. Their companionship, warmth, and friendliness made writing this book a joyful experience.

Pam Edins, who edited the first draft of the manuscript.

Sarah Lopez and Frank Ostrowski, who reviewed all my notes and proofread the manuscript and made valuable suggestions. I greatly appreciate their love, caring, and friendship.

Joan Haywood, Valarija Mesaros, Malkanthi and Asoka Jayasundara, Maryline and Ron Pumphrey, Amy Lamotte, David and Karen Christians, and everyone else who supported me in bringing this special gift to the world.

The Message of
the Lotus

The gift of truth excels all other gifts.

THE BUDDHA

Behold the splendor of the sunrise as a new day dawns!

The view of the early morning sun rising over the horizon is always exhilarating. However, if we live on the western side of a forest, the beautiful sunrise is not available to us unless we take the time to walk around or through the woods and across swampy marshes. Then we can partake of the splendor of nature's creation.

Some mornings, though, a thick mist forms over the lake, obstructing the magnificent view of the rising sun. Even on these mornings, we know that the sun still shines with the same luster beyond the transient mist. In spite of the woods, in spite of the mist, the glory and the essence of the sun remain.

So, the eager among us venture to climb the mountain that rises above the mist. Then, to our supreme joy, we find that we have trodden the path that guarantees us the pristine beauty of the sunrise every day, with not even the mist to stand in between. Self-determination, courage, and genuine effort to conquer the obstacles of the woods and then the mist were all we needed to enjoy that reward.

The story of our human existence is no different from the sunrise. There is inherent beauty and magic to human life, the flagship of nature's wonder. It is fascinating to be a human being, and each one of us is a miracle. In the magnificent, complex architecture of life on this planet, human life is the lustrous sun. The glorious essence of the human being is always present within each one of us, just like the sun, even though sometimes it cannot be seen. To reach it, we need to work on overcoming what stands in between.

As we know, it is not easy to be human, or rather, to be with our essential beauty. The human experience has its woods and mists. Life is full of challenges, difficulties, and struggles. Moments turn into hours, days into months, and years into decades as we wish, wait, and yearn for more. When we understand how truly fleeting life is, we ask, "Is there meaning in all of this? Is there a purpose to life? Where and to what does it lead?"

How often do you feel that something is missing in your life? How often do you sense the intense desire to release yourself from the loneliness and emptiness that you feel at times for no apparent reason? How often do you feel a longing for something greater, something as yet undefined? Where can you find fulfillment, happiness, and peace?

We hear about rare individuals who have taken the

trouble to "walk through or around the woods," have discovered the answers to such existential questions, and have "seen the sunrise" of life and experienced the awakening of their heart. At a spiritually higher level, some have even climbed above the mist to be with the pristine beauty of the sunrise every day. They have realized the inherent, highest essence in the human being, which is clear, beautiful, and always intact, in spite of what may obscure it. They have experienced serenity. They have found peace. They *are* peace and serenity.

We call these individuals spiritually awakened people, saints, or enlightened beings. Some of us are eager to follow their path and reach the same destination. And we can. All we have to do is take the trouble to walk around or through the woods, as they did. And when our spiritual ambitions become even higher someday, we can climb the mountain to see above the mist. There is no other way. It is called the spiritual path.

In this book, it is my intention to share with you what I have gleaned from the path trodden by one of these extraordinary individuals: the Buddha. I will also tell you about experiences from my life on the long walk I have undertaken to see the sunrise. It is my earnest and sincere hope that you will be a fellow traveler on the path.

My own initiation to the spiritual path happened in a rather incidental way. I was a boy of thirteen, growing up in a small village in Sri Lanka. I was a very energetic and active young teenager, somewhat mischievous, too, as were many other boys my age. Whether because of these qualities or not, I also happened to be my father's favorite son. Being born into a Buddhist family, I had developed a veneration for things Buddhist, including the saffron robe. I had a notion that monks command respect and are wise. However, my knowledge of, and interest in, Buddhism or spirituality at the time was the same as my knowledge of Einstein's theory of relativity: I knew it existed, but much was beyond my grasp.

For a Buddhist family to have a young son enter the monastic tradition is a great honor as well as an emotionally painful sacrifice. My parents sent my older brother to the temple, as his nature seemed to fit monastic training. However, upon examining the reports derived from our horoscopes, the chief priest found that the one best suited for the holy path was not my brother but me, and he appealed to my father to allow me to enter monastic life. So, with the only tears I had ever seen in his eyes, my father dispatched me to the temple.

When I completed my first year of training, I was ordained as a novice monk. After the initial period of anticipating great things passed and I faced the "real life" of a young monk, I found the transition to be very difficult. To begin with, as soon as I observed the Ten Precepts (disciplinary rules for monks) and wore the saffron robes, the laity treated me as a holy man; the fact that I was still in a teenager's body didn't seem to matter at all to them. Most uncomfortable was when my parents, sisters, and brothers (including the brother with whom destiny made me switch the vocation of monkhood) bowed down or knelt at my feet in the customary Buddhist way to show respect. It took me a long time to accept the fact that it was the Buddha and his teaching, the *dharma*, that they showed respect to, *through* me as the Buddha's messenger. Then I began to feel more comfortable with the ritual.

Traditionally, ordination implies a full commitment to follow the spiritual path of the Buddha. At a certain point in the ordination ceremony, I held in my hands the robes I would eventually wear and recited a verse in Pali, an ancient language in which the original Buddhist scriptures were written. The meaning of the verse was to dedicate my life to the spiritual path, to overcome all the pain and suffering in life, and ultimately to achieve perfect peace by awakening to the ultimate reality of Nirvana. Upon reciting the verse, I respectfully requested that my teacher take the saffron robes and ordain me.

If I, from the vantage point of a thirteen-year-old, had understood the real meaning of what I was saying and the enormous responsibility it would impose upon me, I would have run away and never become a monk. However, looking back on my life from where I stand today, I am glad that I didn't know the real meaning that day. Now I wouldn't trade my life as a monk for anything else.

During the early days of search and discovery my teenage years passed quickly, as I was busy learning, teaching, performing rituals, and taking care of temple affairs. However, as I began to feel overwhelmed by my daily responsibilities as a novice and by the pain of separation from my family, especially my mother, I almost ran away from the temple on at least two occasions. Open-minded, curious, at times restless, and even openly rebellious, I observed the temple life for nine years. With my inquiring mind, I became interested in other spiritual teachers and masters from non-Buddhist traditions as well. Then came the time to test my wings.

At the age of twenty-two, I left Sri Lanka and became a different kind of seeker. Without knowing exactly what I was searching for, I traveled for three years in Asia—in Thailand, Malaysia, Burma, India, and Nepal. Traveling a little over a year in India and Nepal, I visited temples, gurus, ashrams, yogis, holy shrines, and any and every place and person I heard to be spiritual. Unlike any other Theravada Buddhist monk known to me, I sang devotional *bajans* with gurus, practiced yoga with *sadhus,* sat in silence with yogis, and felt at home with spiritual teachers of non-Buddhist traditions in India. (I attribute my attraction for yogis and my comfortable feeling with them to having been a yogi myself in one of my former lives.)

I took many lonely, and sometimes long, silent retreats in my travels. There was a time when I was taking at least one day a month to observe silence for twenty-four hours. Given the benefits I have experienced from this practice, I still try once in a while to do it, in spite of my busy travel schedule.

A momentous change occurred in my life at age twenty-five, when I moved from Asia to North America. This was also the time my dear mother left this world, and, to my greater sorrow, I received the news a month after she passed away. I spent two years at a temple in Canada, after which I returned to what I like most—spreading spirituality as a traveling monk, through the combined roles of teacher, friend, student, and seeker. Although I set off on my travels in the formal role of teacher, I always feel as though I am a student in the classroom of the world, because I learn so much from each encounter I have with another human being.

This commitment requires extensive travel, which takes me to many parts of the world, a level of mobility quite uncommon for a Buddhist monk today. The world has become my home, and all the people I have met are members of my large extended family. I have become a citizen of the world.

During my travels around the world, I have had the opportunity to live as a guest with hundreds of local families in many countries. And I have stayed with people across the whole spectrum of living conditions, from those with the greatest luxury and comforts to those with the worst deprivation and suffering. I have had opportunities to share deep moments and close feelings with the rich and the poor, the young and the old, the educated and the uneducated, white people and those of color. I have traversed these seemingly impenetrable barriers of culture because I strongly believe that real spiritual strength does not recognize cultural boundaries, identities, and labels. I spend more of my time with Christians, Hindus, Moslems, Jews, and those of other religions than with Buddhists—admittedly rather unusual for a Buddhist monk.

I became a teacher the day I was ordained. Buddhists consider all their monks, be they young or old, as their teachers. Yet now I know that to become a good teacher it takes much more than the robes, precepts, and ordination. It takes diligent work and courageous commitment to my own spiritual journey. As the essence of the teachings of the Buddha inspires me deeply, the compassion that results from it makes it easier to help others by sharing what I know and what I have.

If we can develop an open mind, an ever-present curiosity, and a desire to learn, if we can cast aside self-made barriers and think of all fellow human beings as brothers and sisters, and if we can experience the entire world as our home, we will have walked around the woods and marshes to see the sunrise of life. As we pass the marshes, we must take the time to appreciate the essential beauty of our surroundings. A marsh is dirty and full of weeds. It may be replete with algae and froth. It is not something that invites a second look from a passerby. Then, one day, there appears the bud of a water plant, hardly noticeable. Days later, something in the marsh attracts the attention of the passerby. For the first time, he stops by the marsh. He gazes at a flower of pristine beauty that has blossomed from the water plant. The marsh, with its unappealing froth, algae, and weeds, is no longer visible to him—he sees only the beauty and pure essence of the lotus blossom.

Our wholesome essence, the Buddha-nature within, is similar to the essence of the lotus. In spite of the weeds and dirt surrounding it, the lotus flower still blossoms, outshining everything around it. A lotus is a lotus. All that matters, all that is effective, all that shines, and all that is seen is the pristine beauty of its blossom.

In my daily life I try to remember the message of the beautiful lotus. Though grounded in the mud and surrounded by murky water, it grows out of, and beyond, the impurities that surround it, reaches the sunlight, and blossoms into a beautiful flower. The lotus has taken a long path through the mud and the murky water, seeking the sunrise to open its heart to the world and express its essence.

I have made a commitment to follow the example of the lotus. The lotus has become my auspicious symbol and represents the potential purity of heart and unconditional love that I can radiate. I have made it my mission to help others grow as the lotus did.

So in our efforts to see the sunshine, we walk through or around the woods. We pass by the marshes, noticing the beautiful lotus and realizing the profound message it is trying to convey to us to mold our own lives. Having crossed over to the side where the sun rises, we realize that, with a little more effort, we can climb to the mountaintop, where even the occasional patch of mist will not take away the magnificent view of the sunrise. Join me and be my fellow traveler. As we walk, let me tell you what I have discovered along the journey thus far.

At this point, and before we go into the remaining chapters, let me brief you regarding the way the chapters that follow are organized. Each chapter opens with questions and a quick meditation on what your preconceived notions about the upcoming theme are. After you have asked and answered these questions, quiet your mind, be peaceful and open, and read each essay without prejudice, without attempting to compare what you read with your earlier notions. Comparison should be done only after the new ideas have been properly understood.

CHAPTER TWO

The Path

To see the world in a grain of sand,
And Heaven in a wild flower,
Hold infinity in the palm of your hand
And eternity in an hour.

WILLIAM BLAKE

ASK YOURSELF

Life is sacred. *That sacredness manifests itself as our inner essence, the divinity or the potential for enlightenment. It is ever present within each and every human being, although we may not be conscious of it.*

Have you had a moment to extend your vision of life beyond the appearance of body and mind, to experience that pure essence?

We should love, respect, and nurture all *life. That process needs to begin with yourself, because your life is representative of the life force within each and every living being. We know that it is harder for those who are not in touch with their inner pure essence to respect or nurture themselves. How serious are you in seeking and actualizing your inner essence so that it will bloom into your liberating experience? Did you ever think about where you should begin the journey? What kind of guidance, instructions, or tools are you going to need to clear the path?*

Think of babies or very young children for a moment. Aren't we all attracted to their purity, happiness, innocence, playfulness, and special radiance? Could that be because their inner essence is more active, resulting in genuine spontaneity? Can you identify any of their qualities that you would like to see in adults? And in yourself?

Now that I have you thinking, let us move on.

THE INNER ESSENCE

I am convinced that human beings are provided with the foundation and potential necessary for spiritual growth and awakening. It is our birthright. As we come into this world, nature endows us with a wholesome essence on which to build a meaningful, enjoyable life, with no limits to what we can do. We only have to know and believe in our inherent spiritual essence and wholeness, then choose to use them to open our hearts. I strongly believe in our inner essence and our ability to reach it, not just theoretically, but because many experiences in my life have led me to this conclusion.

As we grow up, some of the innate purity and goodness of youth gets buried or veiled. As the Buddha said, "The mind is pure and luminous by nature. It is defiled only by adventitious thoughts and emotions." Fortunately for us, however, as the Buddha's great gift to us, he left behind practical methods that will enable us to revive and use the pure mind, as we will discover in the lessons throughout this book. These methods, since their initial discovery by the Buddha, have been proven, time-tested, and used by millions of the Buddha's followers over the last 2,500 years.

First, a recollection from my own experiences to illustrate our endowed essence: I was very fortunate to have lived for a while with a wonderful family who had a three-year-old daughter named Sasha. In their home, a room was set aside just for meditation. This room was furnished simply, creating an aura of holiness and serenity. I used the room regularly for my own meditation, typically once in the morning and once in the evening.

One day as I was meditating with my eyes closed, I sensed someone else in the room, although there was no discernible sound to indicate that someone had entered. I opened my eyes, and whom did I see? It was Sasha with her eyes closed, seated by my side, legs folded into the half-lotus posture, a miniature replica of myself. I smiled and very softly said, "Hello." Sasha opened her eyes and looked at me apologetically. I smiled again to reassure her it was okay for her to be there, and then I closed my eyes and returned to my meditation. Sasha remained silent until I finished.

Another day Sasha followed me into the meditation room, and for a few minutes we talked about what I do when I meditate. She asked me why I sit still and close my eyes. I explained to her that it is to make myself feel peaceful. I explained a few more things about meditation in simple language that she could understand. During this time, I could see she was listening with immense interest and curiosity. I asked her if she wanted to meditate with me. She was thrilled with the invitation, and she promptly positioned herself in the half-lotus posture before I could even lower myself to the floor.

We sat with our eyes closed, and I first counted to ten to correspond to ten breaths. In the beginning, ten counts was just about how long she was able to maintain her stillness. After practicing for a few days, she could maintain it longer.

One summer day we were all in the dining room having lunch. Having finished hers earlier, Sasha decided to go play in the backyard. Although we could see Sasha through the open window, we did not pay much attention to her as we continued eating. After some time we noticed that Sasha was being a little too quiet, so we looked out the window. There she was, sitting in the meditative position under a big tree, her eyes closed and head lowered, exactly like in the meditation room. Everything was quiet, and she looked absolutely serene and peaceful.

I was so intrigued by what I saw. Without thinking and without realizing that I was being an intruder, I stepped out and casually asked, "Sasha, are you meditating?" Although I asked the question, perhaps I presumed that a three-year-old child was not capable of meditating seriously. Little Sasha proved me wrong. She slowly lifted her head and, giving me a compassionate look, softly whispered, "Yes." Then she lowered her head back to its original position and began to meditate again. This was a beautiful experience for me. For a brief moment, the innocence, purity, and peace in her eyes lifted me to a higher spiritual level. I slowly walked back into the house again. Looking through the window, I could see her meditating for a few more minutes. Then she came back into the house to join us.

In these and many other spontaneous, natural, and unadulterated behaviors I have encountered with Sasha as well as other children, I have discovered many virtues, among them curiosity, openness, kindness, respect for life, honesty, serenity, and spontaneous joy. When I observe very young children, as one keenly interested in spirituality, I can't help but come to two conclusions:

First, we desire to be happy. To be happy means to live in a world where we can feel serene, be joyful, grow in knowledge, and have pleasant experiences. When we observe very small children, such as my friend Sasha, we see that they have these key qualities.

Second, somewhere along the way something happens to these virtues, and as a result, many of us are either not happy or not as happy as we could be. In Buddhism, we believe that these qualities are still there, but, like rust that forms on metal with the passage of time, impurities have covered them.

In spiritual terms, we can say that the inner essence is always within us. The essence is pure and unadulterated. Now, in order to see it we need to remove the rust. But what exactly is this rust? It is nothing but the accumulated conditionings received from cultural, social, religious, and other influences during our growing years. How we remove the rust will be discussed later in this book.

This does not mean that we should yearn to be children again. That would be meaningless and foolish. Rather, we should be proud to be adults, yet recognize the importance of regaining *some* of the wholesome qualities that nature intended us to retain throughout our lives. Once we regain these qualities, they should be complemented with others that are special to adulthood, thereby creating the foundation needed to reach the happiness we desire.

While worldly happiness is easily understood and is in fact what we normally yearn for, it is important to understand that there is a higher level of spiritual happiness that is attainable by the human mind because we are provided with an enormous capacity for development. However, except for a few extraordinary human beings, this capacity goes largely unused. By using certain proven techniques of mind development, we can activate the dormant capacities and realize a level of extraordinary spiritual achievement—that of an enlightened being. It is because this potential exists in all of us that we say the Buddha-nature is within us, but we need to realize it. Like the lotus in the marsh, we need to eventually see its blossoming.

ALONG THE WAY

Let us try to identify some of the qualities that we're already endowed with at the beginning but which we often lose along the way. When we look closely at them, we can understand how these simple qualities, which express the pure spiritual nature, were within us when we were little children.

Learning from mistakes. When we were very young, our mistakes were our greatest learning tool. For example, as we were learning to walk, if we stood up the wrong way or took an incorrect step, we fell. And each time we fell, we tried again, and gradually we mastered the art of walking. We grew up only because we made mistakes, learned from them, and discovered how to do things right.

Unfortunately, along the way we were told that it is bad to make mistakes. We began to lose the initial enthusiasm we had for trying new things because we feared punishment for making mistakes, or we lied when we made a mistake, which created guilt. So we have lost the most effective tool for growth. Learning from mistakes is a classic example of a quality that nature intended us to retain all the way throughout life. If we are to move rapidly through the process of spiritual evolution and find the happiness we are seeking, we need to reclaim this tool.

Curiosity. When we were young, we were intrigued by every new thing that crossed our path. We would stop to smell a flower when we walked in the woods or to gaze at a strange formation of stars in the sky. Now we have no time for such things, or we think they are not important.

As children, we used to ask questions of those around us about anything that we did not know. Now we dare not, because others may laugh at us. We were awed by everything new that we encountered, and we experimented enthusiastically till we knew why and what and how. Sometimes that learning process was hindered by meaningless intervention from well-intentioned people around us. Let me tell you a story that illustrates this point.

I was sitting in the living room of a friend's house reading a book. Her daughter was playing in a corner of the room. Suddenly I heard the mother shouting, "No, no, no!" and running over to her. The mother continued to shout, and soon the little girl was crying hysterically. I walked over to see what had happened.

The child had picked up a pin from the floor. The mother had seen that and, fearing her daughter might put the pin in her mouth, panicked, ran to the little girl, and forcibly took the pin away. Obviously, the mother had the child's welfare at heart. At the same time, though, I could see that the little girl was hurt emotionally.

I very nicely asked the mother to give the pin back to her daughter. The mother was surprised. She thought I was out of my mind and refused to give the pin back. After many requests from me, she finally, but reluctantly, handed the pin back to her daughter.

Now the little girl was very happy, as I could see from the sparkle in her eyes. She also stopped crying. I sat down beside her and asked if I could see what was in her hand. I acted curious about what was in there. She stretched out her palm and showed me the pin. After talking to her for a little while, I held out my own hand and asked her to put the pin in my palm. Reluctantly she did. Then, to show that she could trust me, I gave the pin back to her. We played for a little longer and then I "made the pin disappear." We both looked for it but could not find it. A little later, in a friendly way, I explained to her about the dangers of playing with things like pins and how we must be careful when handling them.

When I had the opportunity to talk to the mother away from the child, I cautioned her that children's psychological growth can be stunted and their curiosity dampened if we are not careful. I also told the mother how such safety precautions can be explained to a child in a different and peaceful way that won't destroy the child's curiosity. Curiosity is essential growth material for the mind, and its fruit is wisdom and, later, spirituality. It must be nurtured rather than suppressed.

Honesty. We do things based on truth. Somewhere along the way we get into trouble for telling the truth or acting on truth. Then gradually we learn that we succeed in avoiding similar trouble by deviating from truthfulness. Not for long, though. If we continue with dishonesty, then things start backfiring until our life gets totally "sticky." Honesty pays in the long run, and now we want to find out how to get back to where we started.

Love. When we were very young, we loved other beings unconditionally. If the other person did not return our love, we did not react with anger or hatred. Love was never associated with fear. It was spontaneous and arose from a pure heart. Love was not discriminatory. We loved the baby-sitter, the gardener, and our brothers and sisters simply as human beings. Again, somewhere along the way we lost that purity as a result of external influences. Then we began to love with discrimination.

A child always has an innate affinity toward his or her parents and to the other people around them. Sometimes a child may be a little self-conscious and shy at the beginning when interacting with a stranger. Yet, given the proper opportunity for them to get to know the stranger, they can easily love that person as much as they would a parent. I have played with children from all around the world, and I'm fortunate to have had the opportunity to stay with hundreds of families and interact with their children. Draped in an orange robe, I know how different and strange I may appear to children in Russia, North America, or Europe. However, as I extend my friendship to them, I have found that often it takes no time at all to experience their love.

At the Omega Institute in Rhinebeck, New York, where I teach every summer, one week is designated Family Week. Many children come to Omega that week. Family Week is one of my favorite times of the year. During that period, I teach a meditation class to children. One summer, at the end of Family Week, an Omega staff member came to me and asked, "Bhante Wimala, you were a great hit this week. Children really love you. What is your secret?" I answered, "Children are truly beautiful beings. I love them. They easily respond to love." She walked away with a big smile.

We always want our love to be returned in equal or higher doses by the recipient. If not, we often follow up with action that we think will bring that love to us but which, ironically, creates a greater distance in the relationship. Once again, if we want to progress along the spiritual path, we have to reclaim the attribute of *unconditional* love.

The qualities mentioned above and many others, such as trust and respect, desire to explore, spontaneity, simplicity, and creativity, are all qualities that are not reserved exclusively for a child. They have no age barriers and they were meant to last a lifetime. Unfortunately we lost them, or some of them, along the way, and we need to reclaim them if we are to progress onward to a happy and spiritually fulfilling life.

RECLAIMING NATURE'S GIFTS

In trying to reclaim these wholesome qualities, we need to be aware that not only are they fully or partially submerged, but each quality is covered by its unwholesome counterpart. For example, if the natural quality of unconditional love is suppressed in someone, invariably there is hatred covering the dormant quality of pure love. Likewise, if an individual does not treat mistakes as opportunities for growth, then there will be a tendency to blame others or oneself, which usually is accompanied by anger or guilt. And anger or guilt can take us away from the natural spiritual center within.

Our restorative work is two-pronged. First, we have to work on gradually eradicating any unwholesomeness that has taken root along the way—for example, hatred or jealousy. Second, we have to uncover and nurture the original wholesome quality. These two complementary goals can, in some cases, be achieved through an integrated practice. As an example, one method of gradually overcoming hatred and uncovering and nurturing unconditional love is to practice the loving-kindness meditation. That technique is explained in a later chapter.

In order to restore wholesome qualities, we need to work diligently. The amount of work needed will depend on how obscured a particular unwholesome quality is, and how strong and deep its unwholesome roots are.

Once we are successfully on a path of reclaiming lost or suppressed childhood qualities, we also need to nurture the adult qualities that naturally grow within us.

One example of an adult attribute is self-reliance. Infants by nature are totally dependent on others for their survival. It is also natural for this particular helplessness to disappear as we grow older and stronger.

As we grow into adulthood we have the potential to develop our independence and self-reliance in place of dependency. Note that I said "potential." If we do not take the needed action to develop our self-reliance, then we could continue to be dependent on the outside world in the way an infant or child is. Of course, the consequence of not developing self-reliance would be a lack of happiness and peace. The dependent adult causes misery to himself or herself as well as to those he or she is dependent on.

Responsible adults whose interest extends freely beyond the confines of self enjoy a happiness unique to adulthood. However, those lost on the journey from childhood to adulthood can also totally reclaim the lost happiness of adult life. The potential energy of these wholesome qualities is what carries them to a high level of happiness and peace and allows them to reach their spiritual goals.

JOURNEYING TO THE HIGHER PEAKS

Let us assume for a moment that we have reached the level of happiness that we ordinarily aspire to. In this state, we are content with our lives.

Our minds are generally calm and peaceful. We have no fears or worries, because we do not feel threatened by other people or events or circumstances. We do not become enraged with others, because we have learned to accept errors, mistakes, and deficiencies in the world as a normal part of existence. We do not erupt with jealousy due to feelings of inadequacy, thinking that others are more privileged than we are. Whether others are acting toward us in a pleasant way or not, we can maintain our composure fairly well. While we feel free, we conduct ourselves in a way that does not obstruct the freedom of others.

Having reached this state of happiness, can we say that

we have reached the ultimate goal potentially available to human beings? Most unlikely. Consider for a moment the following.

Many great sages over the years have said that as humans we ordinarily reach only a fraction of our full potential. They say that in using only a small portion of the mind's capacity, we live at a "worldly" or "mundane" level, and even the happiness described above is still mundane. Today's scientists echo the same view when they say that human beings use only a very tiny percentage of the brain's capacity, quoted variously at figures less than 10 percent.

Suppose we were able to harness a good portion of the unused 90 percent or so of our brain's (or the mind's) capacity, and direct that power for spiritual attainment. Now imagine what a higher level of happiness we would be able to reach. The sages of the past spoke of this level of happiness as "supermundane" (beyond worldly) happiness. It would be so different from our present idea of happiness that we would not even refer to it as happiness. Buddhists call this higher state the bliss of Nirvana.

The way to this higher level of happiness, beyond ordinary or mundane happiness, is through meditation. Meditation, as practiced in Buddhism, is subdivided into development of tranquility (*samatha*) and development of insight (*vipassana*).

Samatha is what enables us to sharpen our minds for use beyond their present level. *Samatha* may be compared to a fluorescent lamp in a room that was earlier illuminated by candlelight. The lamp helps us to see things better.

Vipassana, or insight meditation, enables us to see

beyond appearance or mundane reality. In other words, it enables us to see truth or perceive things as they really are. A mind that is capable of seeing truth with perfect insight is able to experience supermundane happiness.

The peace, happiness, and meaning that we seek is already available and accessible within each one of us. Discovering them through awakening, and experiencing them, is the work of our spiritual path. It is the path of spiritual self-discovery. Whether you are climbing the smaller mountains of the Himalayas to look at the beautiful valleys or reaching for the peak of Mt. Everest to experience the breathtaking view, only your own steps can take you there. The path to happiness and highest peace must be trodden by each of us, alone. No other person can walk this path for you. The Buddha's teachings, which have guided his diligent followers to the mountain peak of spirituality, repeatedly remind the novice seekers thus: "You yourself must walk the path. Buddhas merely show the way."

How genuinely committed are you to being a traveler on the path to happiness and supreme freedom? Are you prepared and willing to commit the needed effort for your own salvation?

CHAPTER THREE

One Day at a Time

Look to this day!
For it is life, the very life of life.
In its brief course
Lie all the verities and realities of your existence:
The bliss of growth;
The glory of action;
The splendor of achievement;
For yesterday is but a dream;
And tomorrow is only a vision;
But today, well lived, makes every yesterday
a dream of happiness,
and every tomorrow a vision of hope.
Look well, therefore, to this day!

KALIDASA

ASK YOURSELF

Just skim the following paragraphs for a few seconds and make
a mental note to come back to them when you wake up tomorrow

morning. *When the morning arrives, spend some quiet time relaxed and contemplative and try to absorb the meaning and message contained in these paragraphs.*

Think about how you want to spend the new day ahead of you. It has eighty-six thousand seconds. Think of it as eighty-six thousand dollars. Do you want to spend it wisely and work toward creating eventual wonders in your life? Or do you want to gamble with it and waste it?

Linger a little while in bed and cast away all the usual thoughts of the daily tasks that lie ahead. Instead, gently gaze around, stretch, and breathe in the day's freshness, the purity of the morning. Then close your eyes and think about the gift of a new day. Let your mind wander from one blessing of the day to another and to another.

Then, when you're ready, open your eyes again. How do you feel about this new day of yours? Observe nature's blessings, be it the sunlight beaming through the window, the sound of the birds, the laughter of children across the street, raindrops pounding on the roof—whatever captures your attention. This is your new day, the chance to spend an entire twenty-four hours just as you wish. Well, now you have rested enough. Arise! There's work to be done if you do not want your eighty-six thousand seconds to slip away.

THE MESSENGER IN DISGUISE

Do you recognize a messenger in these early hours of the morning? Yes, there is a messenger carrying a very important message for you, but it is disguised. The messenger is disguised as none other than your new day. The message it carries reminds you about the sacredness of life and the priceless value of time. This day stands on the memories of yesterday and the dreams of tomorrow. In spite of its immense goodness, it will be here with you but once. Therefore, if you want this day (which will soon be called your past) to be filled with pleasant memories, and your tomorrow to be free of fear, shame, guilt, and worry, pay serious attention to this day.

Each new day arrives bubbling with fresh life. It is here to enliven you if you reach out with eyes willing to see and ears willing to hear. The chirping of the birds, the rays of the sun shining through the window, and the sound of children playing on the street: see, hear, and feel them, all fresh, beautiful, and invigorating, the pulses of the new day.

In the River of Life

In Sri Lanka, we often compare human life to a river. When river water falls down the hills, it creates a beautiful waterfall. When it crashes on rocks, white foam is created, expressing its incredible hidden beauty. When the river silently flows through the valleys, it becomes mysterious and magical. These different things that happen to the river water along its path are all manifestations of its beauty. So, too, if we are to make meaning out of our odyssey as human beings on this planet, we have to accept that whatever happens on our way adds to life's beauty.

We view the rocks of our lives with aversion, but let us learn from the river. In the "eyes" of the river, the rocks add nothing but life to it. Human beings would grumble at the falls (errors, mistakes, failures) of their lives, but the river seems to get a thrill out of its sudden fall, as though it's saying, "Hold on . . . here comes another adventure." Or as it strikes the rocks, like a joyous child it seems to say: "Time to turn into foam again, time to turn into mist this time."

The sound of the fall seems to be music to the river's "ears." Those who live in fear of rocks are bound to miss the soothing, nurturing sounds that have the potential to create beauty.

The river always travels looking for lower ground, seeking to rest in the calmness of the valley. But it has to fall and crash around rocks before it can hope to reach the valley. Without grumbling and complaining, it simply moves on, enjoying all the adventures along the way. Our lives are full of steep falls, rocks, unexpected turns, and surprise encounters. Like the river, we have to move on, accepting that our rocks and falls are all part of the journey, part of the beauty of this river of life. Only if we have the determination to move on with that acceptance can we eventually reach the valley of peace, like that river in Sri Lanka.

GREETING WITH HEART

A wonderful way to share with others the goodness of one's heart is through an honest, friendly, and well-meaning greeting.

We can start the day by greeting ourselves. Why not? A greeting does not always have to be directed toward others. As you look in the mirror for the first time each day, say to yourself mentally or out loud, "Isn't this a gorgeous day! I know I am going to have a wonderful twenty-four hours." Smile warmly to yourself, thrilled that you are alive and able to experience life as a human being.

Next, move on to your immediate family. Having brought a sparkle to yourself earlier in the morning, you can sprinkle that energy on those closest to you. If you are already used to greeting them, has it turned into a mechanical gesture over time? Try to infuse your greeting today with new energy. Let your recipient—whether it's Mom, Dad, your brother or sister, a roommate, or your significant other—feel that your greeting is not an empty vehicle, but comes to them filled with friendliness and love. Try it and see what happens. You may be surprised to discover something new in the air that will last the whole day.

Now, it is also possible that you're not used to greeting those you live with, particularly on an ordinary day like today. After all, it's not Christmas, or Mother's Day, or Grandpa's birthday. It doesn't matter. Just start in a small way by greeting everybody that you know. And then do something different to make that special connection. Look into the eyes of a family member and say something appreciative. Hold their hand and sit still for a minute.

One important note: Don't expect a response from your listeners. If you hear someone mutter, "I don't know what's gotten into you lately," just try to ignore the comment, but diligently keep on with your experiment. Try something similar in the evening, then tomorrow, and then the day after. Very soon you too will discover something new in the air. Very gradually keep increasing the level of intimacy in your greeting, and it will become contagious. Soon you will see a happy family in your own dining room, which will certainly be a big change from the days when Dad read the newspaper while eating breakfast, Mom rushed nervously back and forth between the dining room and kitchen, and the kids gobbled their cereal in three minutes and ran off to watch TV.

Next to the goodness of one's heart, what really adds beauty to a greeting is a smile. What is seen affects us with greater magic than what is heard. So enhance your greeting with a smile. Your smile is a direct connection from your heart to that of the recipient. You can begin the day as a spiritual person by being willing to let yourself share a smile with your family or a friend.

When you greet someone, there is a feeling of respect for that person, due to the sublime realization that he or she is a human being as important as yourself. Never mind what that person does for a living, because that is very insignificant in the order of things. You would greet a beggar on the street with the same respect you would the president of the

United States. In the same way, you can greet a criminal as a human being, but to have the courage to do so one needs to be spiritually strong. Remember, even if you are a "good" person, you have the potential to be a criminal if you stray from your present wholesomeness. Equally, a criminal has the potential to be a good person, if only he or she cares to change for the better and works diligently toward that objective.

As we may expect, there is no better place to look for an example of this divine consciousness (of extending the same respect, love, and compassion to all human beings) than the Buddha's own extraordinary life. The Buddha taught that if we can learn to look beyond mere outward appearances and see into the inner spirit of people, we will be able to respect them and so extend love and compassion toward all human beings regardless of who they are. The fully blossomed selfless, loving heart of the Buddha is aware of the potentiality for a similarly selfless, loving heart within every human being. Any human being who has arrived at that place and acts out of such inner knowing has mastered an essential spiritual strength.

The Buddha, though he addressed kings, noblemen, and faithful seekers, also sought out and taught without discrimination those who were despised, persecuted, or punished for their unacceptable and harmful behavior. Among those he taught were criminals, murderers, prostitutes, thieves, bandits, and socially underprivileged persons. The Buddha knew that the seeds of enlightenment were present in all of them, with no exception.

An oft-quoted example is that of Uppalavanna, a

woman who at one stage in her life was a well-known prostitute. After listening to Buddha-*dharma*, she became a most respected and enlightened nun. Another example is that of a notorious murderer named Angulimala who, again after receiving *dharma* from the Buddha and being enlightened, became one of the greatest psychic healers in Buddhist India. Through these and many other examples, the Buddha taught his disciples that every human being is worthy of respect because they represent the immeasurable wholeness of life.

So, at a higher stage of spiritual evolution, the beggar and the millionaire, the king and the construction worker, the priest and the lay person, the criminal and the saint are all equally worthy of respect. You can welcome each with a respectful greeting. The greeting does not signify approval or disapproval of an individual's behavior, but rather it acknowledges an encounter with a person's life force. This is an extraordinary awareness that can transform the spiritual seeker.

In Sri Lanka, we say *"Ayu bowan,"* which means "May you live long." The words are spoken with the physical gesture of bringing the palms together with the fingers and thumbs touching. In this position, the hands rest on the chest and the head is bent gracefully downward.

Placing both hands on the chest and bending the head forward signifies one's respect for the other person. When done properly, the tradition is very meaningful and nurturing for both giver and receiver. In India people do the same thing by saying *"Namaste,"* which means "I respect you." In the West, this is often translated as "I respect the God-nature within you."

Moving beyond individual differences and recognizing the divinity of human nature is the meaning behind a greeting. It doesn't matter how different we are externally; we are all manifestations of the same universal inner nature. You and I are part of the same cosmic dance, but we may move to two different tunes in a symphony. When we look at our individuality in this light, we will not have to judge another person by his or her movement; instead, we will recognize that we both are moved by the same force—we dance to the same universal symphony.

BEAUTY IS SKIN DEEP

One day when visiting a married couple I have known for a long time, the husband began to complain about his wife taking too much time getting dressed in the morning. He said sometimes she would take as long as forty minutes to get ready, and they were often late for work because of this habit. Quite often they would argue about this, which started the day with bad feelings between them.

With their consent, we sat down to talk about this issue with the objective of finding a practical solution. The wife said, "I want everybody to respect me. When I dress beautifully, my friends and coworkers look up to me. So I feel it's worth taking the extra time in the morning to make myself look nice."

In our sharing, I agreed that one needs to dress nicely and decently. However, I brought her attention to her references to having people "respect" and "look up to" her. If the major goal of changing outward appearance is to gain respect, then when the outward appearance changes, so will the respect. Often, dressing nicely will do very little to command genuine respect. External beauty—your clothing, makeup, and jewelry—may please someone's eyes, but it rarely touches the heart. Probably all of us have heard the saying "Beauty is only skin deep," which refers to how shallow external beauty is. There are some people who do manage to get the *attention* of thousands by showing off their bodies or clothing or jewelry, but how many of them are truly *respected*?

The Buddha taught his disciples—the monks and nuns—to pursue simplicity. Monks shave their heads, wear robes that are always the same color, and live with a minimum of possessions. Having counseled many people whose possessions have been a major cause of dispute and disharmony, I am grateful to the Buddha for his message of simplicity; it has given me a degree of tranquility and peace that I would not trade for any material possessions in this world.

All of this is not intended to suggest that everybody should display the external simplicity of a clergyman. That is not a viable goal for the general population. Rather, what I am advocating here is moderation and balance. While we do need to pay attention to our appearance in order to function in today's society, let's first admit that there is a tremendous overemphasis on appearance.

Actually, only the inner beauty of a person can awaken the spirit of another. Although we may not be conscious of it, we are looking for the other person to recognize our inner beauty. When that connection occurs, it is a comforting feeling.

So I told the wife that if she wants others to truly respect her, she needs to work on both inner and outer beauty. I suggested she spend twenty minutes getting dressed and ten minutes meditating, leading herself into a peaceful and loving state. It is like dressing your spirit with diamonds. The beauty of this spirit will be seen only by the people who truly appreciate you, who are the ones who matter. When your spirit begins to shine and the qualities of your heart begin to surface, you will not worry so much about external beauty.

Fortunately, I don't have to worry about what I should wear every morning. All my robes are the same color and length. In the West, I look visibly different, like a mango in a basket of apples. So when I travel in this part of the world, people often stare at me, sometimes with astonishment. It is not only children (whose natural curiosity is understandable) who stare at me but also adults.

Once while I was waiting at an airport in Texas, I noticed an older man staring at me. With my dark skin, shaved head, and orange robes, surrounded by men and women in business suits, I was very conspicuous. In recognition of the constant attention he directed toward me, I smiled and nodded at him. After a few minutes, he walked over to me and said very loudly, "You look really strange." I smiled at him again, not quite knowing what to say. Finally I said, "Yes, I know." "Well," he snorted, seemingly satisfied with himself, "then why don't you change?"

I smiled yet again and told him that I look the way I do because I am a Buddhist monk, a representative of one of the world's major religions, and that many people accept my appearance as that of a clergyman. He seemed pleased with this explanation, and we spoke for a few minutes. I told him that in Asia monks who dress like me are quite common and can be seen everywhere. I noticed how his curiosity and judgment faded away. Now we were talking like two men, both from planet Earth, and he began to feel comfortable with me. It has been my experience that when I show people my kindness and understanding about their judgments, we tread the trail of peace toward overcoming "social" barriers.

When I speak to children in schools, I often remind them that behind skin colors, clothes, sizes, and shapes there are real people who are just like them—something we should try to remember always. We should respect everybody because they are all human beings—not more, not less.

Think of Mahatma Gandhi or Mother Teresa. Mahatma Gandhi wore only a small piece of handmade cloth and had minimal belongings. Yet millions of people respected him and still do. Why? And why do they respect Mother Teresa? Have you ever seen her wearing makeup or expensive clothes? Although we are not Mahatma Gandhis or Mother Teresas, the same spiritual principles that have brought them respect and love can work in our lives, too. Simplicity and humility are powerful spiritual qualities for everyone.

REFLECTION

Let us reflect on some of the key points we just discussed.

Respect is something that you earn. It is a natural response from others to something good and beautiful about you. Look at yourself closely for a moment. Reflect on the level of respect you receive from others and how you feel about it. Are you happy with it? If you are not, can you see why you don't get the respect you desire?

Are there any qualities in your personality that make it hard for others to offer their respect to you—for example, in the degree of attention you pay when you listen to people, your own selfish attitude toward others, the extent to which you care about them, and the level of genuine love you radiate? Think of a few changes that you could make in your personality and attitude in order to earn real respect from others. Follow your intentions with a commitment for action.

We all like to be noticed and appreciated. For that we seek attention from others. What do you notice about your need for attention? Do you crave a lot of attention, particularly in relationships? If so, identify the persons from whom you desire such attention. How does that desire interfere with having harmonious relationships? Ask yourself if you are overemphasizing your external appearance for the sake of getting attention, at the expense of developing your mind and spirit.

Now, make a commitment to yourself to try for one month not to depend on others' attention in order to feel self-worth. See if you can simplify, or cut down on, the things you do to enhance your external appearance for the purpose of seeking attention. Instead try to cultivate positive, spiritual qualities that are naturally attractive to others. At the end of the month, reflect on your relationships and see if you notice a change. Also note its effect on your feelings and self-esteem.

GRATITUDE

Even if someone gives you only a spoonful of rice, be grateful" is a Sri Lankan saying. The great spiritual masters, especially the Buddha, considered gratitude to be a great virtue, one that helps everyone's spiritual growth. The first thing to be grateful about is the blessing of the new day. This means to appreciate life in all its wonder and beauty. It also means totally accepting yourself for who you are, as well as the world around you, which is here to support you. We usually tend to measure that support by the quantity or worth of our material possessions.

I often come across people who tell me they have nothing to be grateful about. My immediate response to them is that they can start by being grateful for each breath they take. Then there is the sunrise and the sunset and the sunshine in between, which supplies the energy that keeps us ticking. Then the trees, the birds, the lakes, and so on and so on in an endless list. It is difficult for me to understand or accept people's saying that there is nothing to be grateful about.

We are alive because many forces existed and continue

to exist in a caring, harmonious, and delicate balance to support life. Even if you are the poorest person in the world, there is, above all else, this life-giving and life-supporting essence to be grateful about.

At one time I was traveling alone in India on a pilgrimage and I didn't have much money. I was visiting spiritual teachers such as gurus and yogis and staying in ashrams. I didn't have any plans as to exactly where I was going, nor was there any time limit on my journey.

One day I ended up in a small coastal town in eastern India. I befriended a fisherman who allowed me to stay in a small hut made out of palm leaves. By then I had just ten rupees left, a very small amount of money. My only other possession was a small suitcase in which I carried my robes, toilet requisites, and travel documents. I was in a foreign country, I had been away from my family and friends for almost three months, and I didn't know the local language except for a few words that helped me to get by. At that moment, my only companion in transit was the fisherman who was kind enough to let me stay in the hut. I didn't know exactly where I was going next. If I wanted to worry, there were many things to worry about, so I chose not to. Instead, I simply planned to live one day at a time and see what it would bring.

In spite of the smell of the fishing nets, I managed to get a good night's rest while sleeping on the ground. When I awoke early the next morning, the first thought that came to my mind was what my parents or teacher back in Sri Lanka would think if they knew where I had slept that night. It was a most unusual place for a Buddhist monk to sleep. I wondered whether they would be shocked, sad, or angry with me.

After gazing at the thatched palm leaf roof for a few minutes, I got up and walked to the isolated beach, where I did my yoga and meditation. As I was sitting on the beach the sun rose, filling the entire sky with bright and beautiful colors. The waves were lapping on the shore, making soothing musical sounds. The breezes that swept over me moistened my face with the mist of salt water. I was very happy and very grateful to be there. I was grateful for the sun, the sky, the ocean, the breeze, the sand on the beach, and all the beautiful sounds. There were a million blessings all around me. I felt alive and happy.

I wandered along the beach peacefully and happily, expecting to find a small stall to buy some food. I knew that when I'd spent five rupees for breakfast I would be left with only another five rupees for the rest of my journey.

As I was walking along the beach I was surprised to see a white man coming toward me. After all, this was not a tourist beach. As we got closer, to my astonishment (and also to his) we discovered that we were old friends. We remained still for a few minutes, unable to comprehend this most improbable reunion.

About a year prior to this encounter, he had been in Sri Lanka and a friend of mine had introduced us. He had visited my temple several times. Now here I was, running into him in the most unlikely and unexpected of all places on earth—a small fishing village in India.

He put me up in a hotel that night, and the next day we traveled to Bombay together. Before we parted, he gave me more than enough money to continue my journey to my next destination. The important message for me here was to understand that when you appreciate what you have, with genuine gratitude, then what you really need next will come your way effortlessly.

When things get bad, it's easy to become frustrated and feel as though life is nothing but a game of disappointment. I know a lot of people who think they are failures. Once they hold that view, they become angry with themselves. I invite anyone in that dilemma to give deep thought to the fact that he or she is alive, that life as a human being is a miracle, and that this is the greatest gift that can be bestowed in this universe.

GETTING THERE

Usually adult life is laden with routine. With a little awareness and creativity, we can turn these routines into special moments for ourselves and, sometimes, for others as well. Every little awareness and action matters on the spiritual path. One simple action may make a big difference in your life or someone else's, sometimes with lasting effect. Many of us are used to rushing around all the time, and we miss the opportunities to learn and grow. Our actions are the instruments for our growth, and learning from them awakens us spiritually.

Take, for example, a routine drive to and from work. If we examine it closely, we can see that between home and work we have many opportunities to create spiritually meaningful events out of otherwise boring moments. Often we encounter heavy traffic and we simply cannot move as fast as we would like. Sometimes careless drivers cut us off or do other things that aggravate us.

When I sit behind the wheel, I always remind myself to take responsibility for my actions and not to give others control over my moods. I lived in Boston for a while, and there, as in big cities everywhere, the drivers are not known for their courtesy. One day I was pulling out of a metered parking space and a car that was approaching from behind had to stop to let me out because I was already halfway into the street. The driver became quite angry at me for having to stop for a few seconds. He honked and yelled obscenities. I turned around and smiled at him, hoping he would realize that my pulling out in front of him was unintentional. But he got even angrier, banging on the steering wheel and shouting louder.

I felt sorry for him. This man allowed his emotions to get inflamed and to get his blood pressure up because of a few minutes' delay. Who knows how long he would remain angry? I tried to make it easier for him, but he was not receptive. I chose not to let his weakness ruin my day. By choosing not to react angrily and carelessly, I proved to myself that I can refuse to allow someone else's behavior to affect me. I did not feel angry toward him, so there was no pain within me.

Not only did this man refuse to accept my apologetic and positive response, but the way he reacted to it caused him even more turmoil. Those who behave badly usually are eager to see the effects of their behavior on others. They get very disappointed when they see that you are not hurt by their anger. I always tell myself that I want my behavior to be governed by my values, not by others' reactions. Before I get on the road, I prepare myself for objective and calm responses by simply reminding myself to be mindful even as I am commuting. I have found that driving in rush hour does not have to be stressful. On the contrary, it could be a part of my spiritual journey, with many opportunities to exercise my spiritual strength with self-awareness.

ATTITUDE TOWARD YOUR LIVELIHOOD

In some Asian countries, I have met people willing to do any kind of work so that they can feed themselves. I have seen how hard it is for some families to take care of their health without an income. Anybody who has a job is able to find a million reasons to be grateful for his or her livelihood. How often do we look at our livelihood with respect and gratitude? No matter how hard the work is, we should never forget that, apart from the service we provide to others, the work we do also enables us to sustain our lives.

Usually, more than half of one's waking hours are spent on the job, and whatever our state of mind is at work, we carry that over to the rest of our daily activities and even to our home. So it becomes critically important that we strive to maintain peace of mind at our workplace. This can be achieved only by maintaining a proper attitude about the job and its related circumstances.

At work there are supervisors and managers. But to be

responsible for what you do, you need to think of yourself as the boss—not in an organizational way, but in your mind or conscience. Then, when your conscience supervises your work, you gain real satisfaction knowing that you are the responsible master of your self and that you do your work with care and dedication. Your job is transformed from being a mundane routine to becoming a part of your spiritual journey.

One problem that causes a lot of misery for workers is the class system we have created at our workplaces. Ideally, if we need any kind of class division at work, it should be based on the fact that there are skilled and experienced people, who provide guidance, and the unskilled and inexperienced, who receive guidance. The present workplace class systems are based on how workers dress, how much they earn, where one sits in the organizational tree, and other external factors. This system creates artificial barriers so imposing that the president of a company does not dare sit with a laborer in the company cafeteria.

A spiritual person knows that there are no class systems in his or her heart when relating to others, that the different roles are only a structural necessity, purely for the purpose of getting a job done efficiently. When I was in Asia, I thought the caste system there was a social assumption that undermined spiritual fundamentals, basic human dignity, and our sense of respect. Now, living in America, I realize that the class system in the West is not much different, though perhaps not as unbearable.

I cannot see why a doctor, engineer, lawyer, president of a corporation, or any other "respected" professional should be given greater respect than a street cleaner. They all carry the same miracle of human life and deserve the same respect and acknowledgment of dignity.

It must be emphasized that we are talking here not about *recognition*, but about *respect*. By respect, I mean a spiritual acknowledgment of one human being by another human being simply because they are human beings. Undoubtedly, the professional person should be recognized for his or her significantly higher level of education and training, the extra time and energy spent achieving that, and the wider base of knowledge and skills he or she possesses. One obvious way that recognition is shown is in the remuneration paid to the professional. But this recognition should not lead to an inequality in the respect shown to all human beings. That inequality is arbitrary and nonexistent in absolute and spiritual terms. It is driven by society for reasons that boil down to ego, and in practice it manifests itself in the form of differences in attitude and treatment and is unjustifiable.

It's not just the workers with the so-called higher status who perpetuate the class system. Equally responsible are those at the lower end, although their contribution to this class system works at a more subtle level. They are the ones who erroneously feel inferior or less worthy as human beings because they perform work that requires fewer academic qualifications, less pay, less glamorous clothing, and so forth. In other words, they do some kind of work that happens to have been labeled as socially less respectable.

Discrimination is a day-to-day fact in our business and social lives. I urge you to think about recognition and respect and the part they play in your life. If there is confusion between these two, try to resolve it. Regardless of what you do in life, everyone is an equal partner on the journey. As we awaken spiritually, we become better able to overcome the sins of the class system and to recognize everyone as equals. Accepting this equality is an important step forward on our spiritual path.

Contemplate your own livelihood. Do you feel the need to change your attitude? If so, what aspects are important to address, and how would you go about bringing greater harmony into your relationship with your work?

SELF-ACCEPTANCE

As we struggle to cope with the many issues of daily living, it is easy to feel disappointed, disillusioned, and even angry with ourselves. When we feel lonely or frustrated with a situation, we can lose our sensitivity and compassion for ourselves. This in turn can lead to a feeling that we are useless and worthless. We may think of ourselves as failures or victims of life's injustices. That is the time when we most need to work on self-acceptance.

Self-acceptance is creating space in your life so that you can move with ease. Your ability to feel close to yourself is what makes it possible for you to accept yourself for who you are. As you become fully aware of the nature of the actual experience and the underlying causal relationship (Buddhists call this *yoniso manasikara*), you would not fight the experience; rather, you would just accept it.

At the time of a crisis, self-acceptance enables us to relax, let go, and flow with the current rather than fight in panic. With such an attitude, you will find the usual inner resistance, which creates tension, fear, anger, or even aggression, much abated. Self-acceptance will thus help to replace thoughtless reactions with thoughtful actions. It will easily give rise to forgiveness, love, and compassion, making life more peaceful for you. That peace will then radiate to others. My personal experience has taught me a great deal of the wholesome value of self-acceptance. Let me share a simple example with you to illustrate how useful and valuable a tool it is in daily life.

I was traveling to Sweden via Paris. When I reached Paris, I found that my connecting flight was canceled due to an airline strike. There was much chaos in the airport. Many angry, disappointed, and frustrated travelers gathered around the ticket counters. Most of them were complaining, demanding, and arguing with the ticket agents, who were trying to help them. I could see how anger, like an infectious disease, was spreading among the crowd.

As I watched and listened to people and wondered about my own flight to Sweden, growing feelings of frustration began to develop within me. At that point I walked away from the crowd, sat on a chair, and spent a few moments alone, thinking. While it was easy to understand why the ticket holders were angry, I asked myself if it was really necessary to react that way and, for that matter, if this was the only way available for one to react.

I knew it was a time not only for self-acceptance but also for acceptance of the world as it is. I needed to accept that there was a strike and the flight was canceled—there was nothing I could do about them. I also had to accept the fact that such external events do happen in life and that they cause certain feelings within oneself such as I was experiencing at the time. As I began to think in this manner I could feel my mind beginning to calm down. Self-acceptance and acceptance of the world as it is gave me a fresh breath of peace and ease. If only I could have shared my experience of beautiful, peaceful, harmonious feelings with all those who had long, angry faces and disturbed minds—that was the wish that passed through my mind at that time.

I walked up to the counter and smiled at the agent. I let her know that I was aware of her difficult situation and I appreciated her efforts to help everybody. Her face was lit up as she returned an appreciative smile. She even went out of her way and did a special favor for me.

This whole experience was about acceptance, of the world and of the self. I accepted my lot and did what I could to make things easy on my life. I also accepted what was happening in the world outside of me and that the airline personnel did what they could. There was nothing to worry about, no reason for disappointment, and nobody to blame. Whatever the experience is, such unfolding moments carry so much beauty.

When you have deep emotional wounds that have not healed or if you are faced with constant hardships and struggles, it's easy for you to distance yourself consciously or unconsciously from your very own self and feel disconnected. This is almost like shutting the door and walking away from yourself. Then it will be difficult to accept yourself. If you are a spiritual seeker, you need to open the door to welcome yourself again and be closer to yourself in order to get in touch with who you are. As a seeker, you need to observe yourself carefully so that you can know the traps or blocks of emotion that hinder the free flow of your energy. This closeness, observation, and acceptance is essential for inner growth and spiritual awakening.

HOW TO FACE CRITICISM

Criticism is a very common human experience. How often are you shaken by it? Do you normally consider those who criticize you as your enemies? How often do you lose friends because of criticism? Many of us live in fear of being criticized. The Buddha said, "There is no one who is not blamed in this world." Even the most enlightened people are criticized by some. It is obvious that in any society, your ability to face criticism with calmness will lead to success and peace. It is a very important spiritual strength that needs to be nurtured and exercised in your daily life.

The reason we are often intimidated by, or afraid of, criticism is because criticism makes us face ourselves. It sometimes forces us to evaluate our ingrained behavior or beliefs. Criticism is like somebody holding a mirror in front of your face. You must be willing to look carefully before reacting, rejecting, or responding to it. Others provide you with the mirror; if you do not see your reflection there, remove it and respond compassionately. Sometimes, though, you may have to look intently and a few times before you notice what they are helping you to see. Understand that when it's time for you to look at your weaknesses, your eyes have a tendency to get out of focus. That is why you have to make an extra effort to use constructive criticism in a meaningful way.

I always encourage people to criticize my behavior, and I would like to consider those who criticize me as teachers or friends. Wise people know that criticism is a blessing and a lesson to teach them what they can't see in themselves.

Once I received a letter from a friend in Europe and I was surprised by what I read in it. From the beginning to the end, there was nothing but complaints and criticism of me. He wrote that I had acted selfishly when he needed help and that for a Buddhist monk it was not appropriate behavior. After reading the letter, I thought that I should have taken the time to visit with and help him when he really needed me. I had not been aware that he needed me so much, and I had given priority to other commitments. I had honestly forgotten to call and tell him of the changes in my plans that prevented me from seeing him. I now understood that he was disappointed and angry.

Then I telephoned him and thanked him for his letter. My phone call surprised him, and he asked, "How could you call and thank me after I wrote you such a critical letter?" I told him that I understood his feelings and that I had given serious thought to what he had written. I said, "Some of the things that you said might be true, but I did not intend to make you feel that way. At that moment, I thought my other commitments were more important than visiting you. I intended to call you regarding the change in my plans, but with my busy schedule I forgot. Now I understand that visiting you was just as important, and that I missed the opportunity to help you."

I continued, "I did not mean to act selfishly, but, according to your view, it seems that I have acted that way. I owe you an apology and I am very sorry." He said that when he wrote the letter, he had expected to end our friendship, but because of my phone call, there was a new beginning and a better understanding in our relationship.

For those who really want to learn, to grow, and to mature, criticism provides a wonderful opportunity. I take constructive criticism as material for growth, but I don't let it affect my emotions. Of course, there is both constructive criticism and ill-founded destructive criticism. People criticize you with good intentions and sometimes with bad intentions.

Ask yourself, "How am I going to grow if I'm not willing to understand my weaknesses, faults, and inappropriate behavior?" If you're interested in becoming a better person, you must look for your weaknesses. If somebody points them out to you free of charge, be thankful to them for opening your eyes. All you need is the willingness to see.

THE PERFECT WITNESS

Once somebody became very disappointed with me because of a serious misunderstanding. He accused me of something that I had not done. In the beginning, when I first heard the story, I was upset and confused. I felt helpless and didn't know what to do. I had no witness or proof of my innocence. Before long, I discovered the perfect witness: my own conscience. My conscience "talked" to me. Put into words, its message was, "Bhante Wimala, your truth cannot be touched by the lies of this person. Stop struggling with others' lies and remain in touch with the truth known to your conscience. You cannot be hurt or harmed. Your present worry will change to peace."

In the beginning, it was very difficult to convince myself not to be angry. But I listened to the voice of my conscience and I heard it very clearly. After that, it was difficult for me to be upset with that person. I felt at peace.

The story does not end here. Two years passed. Then one day this person came to me and respectfully apologized for the long-past incident. He asked me why I had not made any attempt to prove that he was wrong. Why had I not done anything to stop him, and why wasn't I angry with him now? My answer was very simple. I told him, "You know the truth and so do I. That is all that matters, isn't it?"

Tolerance and patience led us to a renewed friendship. However, to my surprise, one day he brought up the subject again. I told him, "I don't know why you keep bringing up this past incident. It is gone. I don't even think about it anymore." Then he confessed that he still felt guilty about what he had done to me and he wanted to get it out of his system. I told him, "When you were going around telling my friends a lie about me, I knew then that you were doing it to yourself. You don't need my forgiveness because that was already given a long time ago. I think all that remains now to get it out of your system is for you to forgive yourself."

He needed to forgive himself to clear his conscience. We often get into situations that we do not expect or plan, and, willingly or unwillingly, we cause problems for others. When such a thing happens, the spiritual way to handle it is to forgive yourself and make a promise not to do such things again. Take the time to study what errors you made, and look at the emotions you allowed to get the upper hand. View the incident as an opportunity for self-discovery and growth. Confess your guilt to yourself and let yourself go free. Your spiritual life cannot flourish when you keep yourself trapped in the negative energy of guilt.

In day-to-day life, it is not uncommon for people to do "bad" things to us through anger, jealousy, or revenge generated by misunderstanding. These things quite often lead to unfortunate situations. When you face such situations, remember not to act blindly, lose control, or feel helpless. Calm down and look deeply and honestly into your conscience, the witness of your spirit. Take courage and strength from the truth within. Your conscience will be your most caring guardian and trusted friend, though no one else will see it. If you know the truth, you do not have to prove it to anyone else. With your conscience as your closest confidant, you will be at peace.

LIVING THE DAY WITH
SPIRITUAL AWARENESS

Now we have seen some characteristics that make up a typical day for a spiritual seeker. As a spiritual seeker, you can use these ideas to ensure that your own journey is made with greater awareness. Let us summarize some of the important ideas on the path to becoming a spiritual seeker.

- To begin with, greet and welcome each new day as something glorious and try to live that day fully and meaningfully. The day is lived without letting distractions from thoughts of yesterday or tomorrow erode that preciousness.

- You are not fooled by the superficialities of others, nor do you waste your life preoccupied with your own external packaging. You are aware that beauty really is only skin deep. So a greater amount of your time and energy is channeled to develop the inner self.

- You are willing to listen to everyone, but you react to, or integrate into your life, only those views that you evaluate as meaningful. All other things not of value are gently discarded.

- Complaints and problems are only opportunities for learning and growth. Sunshine is wonderful, but so is rain because the water is needed to sustain life. If you venture out, you need only to take an umbrella. Remember the analogy of the river at the beginning of this chapter: Your life can be compared to the river that flows along, uncomplaining of the rocks and the falls. When you choose to live the day with such spiritual awareness, everything encountered is part of the miracle of life.

• Because you are willing to exercise your spiritual awareness, you try to greet the day with joy, with a heart that is full of compassion, gratitude, and love. You view everything you encounter during the day as deserving of its own unique existence. And in being appreciative of everything around you, you are energized, ready to climb the tallest mountains up ahead. You are now a genuine and honest seeker, moving toward your spiritual goal.

CHAPTER FOUR

To Love Is to
Be Free

*Just as a mother would devote her whole life to the care
of her only child, so should one cultivate a concerned
mind toward all beings, without exception.*

GOTHAMA THE BUDDHA

To love or not; in this we stand or fall.

JOHN MILTON, *Paradise Lost*

ASK YOURSELF

*W*hen the radiance of pure love floods our heart, it lights up
*our whole life. As love lifts us into a sublime level of being, that
love overflows and touches others in a special way. We too
experience a great feeling of liberation of the heart. Love is the
most sublime and resplendent beauty of our heart.*

*Let me ask you a few questions regarding your experience
of love and what you have discovered about your capacity to love.*

Recall a moment when you said to somebody, "I love

you," with the strongest feelings. How would you describe your feelings of love toward that person? Go into your personal experience, spend a little extra time on this question, look inside yourself, and try to understand the nature of your feelings of love. Is your experience of love something that you can translate into words?

It is special to be loved. So naturally you would want others to love you. When you say to somebody, "I want you to love me," what do you really expect? Can you describe what you "want"? What do love and loving mean to you?

Are you disappointed about love? If so, could you describe the reason?

Finally, do you think love is a part of being spiritual? Could there be a difference between ordinary love and spiritual love?

THE ELUSIVE UNIVERSAL LANGUAGE

Love is what lifts life above mere existence.

There is nothing strange about love. From the tribal peoples deep in the heart of the Amazon to the movie stars in Hollywood, we all know, or think we know, what it is. Yet it evades clear definition. It is the elusive universal language of mankind.

Love has many faces. It has different meanings to different people in different circumstances. It even encompasses its opposite. For example, hate implies lack of love, and jealousy is a reflection of self-love and other-love in turmoil, with anger often joining in to add fuel to the fire. The subject of love occupies a prominent place in the teachings of great spiritual leaders. For better or worse, love may be considered the most powerful energizer of life. Let us delve into this thing called love, without which life and experience as we know it would cease to exist.

In spite of our preoccupation with love, we seem neither to understand the subject well nor to be in control of it. In fact, it appears that this phenomenon controls *us* according to *its* whims and fancies. When we are driven to the end of our rope, desperate and disillusioned about worldly love, we often turn to spirituality, perhaps assuming that spirituality has little to do with love. Can spirituality exist without love? Or does it encompass love of a kind different from the kind we are running away from? Before we attempt to make sense out of this rather complex emotion, let us make a quiet trip into the recesses of our minds and ponder some Buddhist concepts.

In the language of the Buddha, love is known as *brahma vihara*. *Brahma vihara* means "the godly or divine abode." It is a sublime state of mind. It is the extension and expansion of one's interest beyond all selfish concerns, encompassing the entire universe and all beings without discrimination, exception, or limitation. It is the universal consciousness that transcends self-consciousness. It has been likened to the merging of a river with the waters of the ocean, so that the river loses its identity and becomes one with the ocean.

Love is the experience of the unity of all life. It is the

greatest healer of wounds that people suffer during the struggle for existence. It is sublime because it transcends ordinary, limited, narrow attachment, like the lotus rising above the water. The Buddha called love a "divine abode" because love should become the mind's constant dwelling place, where one feels perfectly "at home."

The effort of the genuine spiritual seeker should be to cultivate love until the mind becomes saturated by it. The mind that has realized the boundlessness of love is nonexclusive and impartial. It is not bound by selective preferences or any prejudices. In order to achieve the goal of this meditative and sublime state of love, the Buddha recommended the practice of meditation called the cultivation of universal selfless love (*metta*).

First Love

Our first experience of love, as we begin our sojourn on this planet, is with our family. It starts with the strong instinctual bonding between children and parents. Caring, affection, and other feelings complement this bond. Next, it extends to encompass others within the immediate family, in particular our siblings, and then it proceeds to cover the extended family.

I grew up in a community in Sri Lanka where warmth and caring for children were abundant. And this love did not abruptly come to an end when I entered adulthood. Rather, a change in closeness was hardly discernible, and emotional support has continued to this day. This is the Buddhist custom of our people.

What I observe in the more economically developed Western part of the world is quite different. Here most people believe that once a person reaches the age of eighteen or so, he is ready to survive on his own. Then the child's relationship with the family often becomes limited to an occasional visit or phone call. Another noticeable factor is the lack of respect and caring of the younger family members for their elders as they grow up. The social structure of the modern world does not allow for anything more than this.

The difference between this scenario and the one in which I was raised became clear to me one day when I was in a classroom with some American teenagers.

When I was a little boy, I used to bow on my knees before my parents every evening before I went to bed. My sisters and brothers did the same. We believe we had a good reason for doing this. Our parents were the ones who took care of our needs. They fed, clothed, and provided shelter for us, and also took care of all our nonmaterial needs, including giving us emotional warmth and support. While we played and studied, they worked hard all day to provide for us.

When I mentioned to the class that I bowed to my parents every day, one of the teenagers stood up and asked me whether I would bow to them even if they were not good parents. When I replied that I would, he was surprised and said that parents should earn respect from their children, and that some parents are not worthy of respect. This time it was I who was surprised, because I have learned that I should not judge my parents.

I replied that my love for my parents was based on a deep sense of gratitude, first for the discomfort and pain my mother had in carrying me for nine months and in giving birth to me, and then for the difficulties both parents had every day in rearing me. In my view, there are no good parents or bad parents. There are just parents who are doing the best they can. The same applies to children. We blame people because we judge them using the standard of perfection.

Each family is unique, as is each individual in this world. No family is perfect and no individual is perfect. There are bound to be shortcomings amid the ups and downs of living. And so it was with the family in which I grew up. I had to suffer some severe discipline at times, which, though I detested it at the time, helped to make me a better person in the long run. As the most important community in my life, my family remained primary and intact, just as expected in that society. My family provided the overall strength and support structure I needed. Like everything else in life, we cannot expect perfection in a family, but we should be grateful if it provides us even the basics of survival in a world where the toughest hurdle *is* simple survival.

So, let us begin by accepting ourselves as we are, and extending this same acceptance to those we grew up with. Where there have been difficulties with family members in the past, let's show new understanding and compassion for them, forgive ourselves and others, and show gratitude for their part in the miracle of our existence.

Then let's move on, leaving the past behind. Neither

parents nor children need to get bogged down as victims of a past that's gone forever. For that matter, Buddhism advises all its followers to "be here and now," that is, live in the present moment, wherein is found reality. All else, both past and future, is a mere figment of the imagination. As we move on, let us remind ourselves once in a while of the price that is paid for not loving. In contrast, let us realize what a wonderful peace is achieved by the givers as well as the receivers when we choose to love with no strings attached.

REFLECTION

Have a friend read this to you, or tape it and play it back, or simply read through it first and then practice:

Close your eyes and relax. Picture your parents. Try to remember how they might have taken care of you when you were a helpless little child, how much trouble they might have gone through to feed and clothe you, take care of your needs, and love you. Remember that they are your origin, your flesh and blood, your beginning and roots.

Now, move your thoughts to yourself as you are today. You may be stronger, richer, or more educated than they. See whether your ego is creating a barrier between you and your parents that keeps you from connecting with them.

Remember how from infancy to the time you left home to be on your own, they were always with you. Recall the good times, such as the times they held you and listened to your hurts and fears; the times they fed you, told you stories, laughed with you, and put you to bed; the times they encouraged you, inspired you, and provided guidance. In your mind, thank your parents and wish them well.

Now recall some of the times that you think were not so pleasant, the days you needed attention and they were in a hurry; the times you needed them and they were not there; the times there was lack of understanding and you felt hurt. Now, from your mature vantage point, try to recognize that all human beings, including your parents, have shortcomings and are entitled to make mistakes, like you. Try to forgive them for their shortcomings and mistakes. Think of your parents not just for their virtues or just for their shortcomings, but as human beings with an entitled mix of the two. Think of them as two beings who, mostly unknown to you, struggled against many hardships and hostile forces to ensure your survival. Thank them, therefore, for your survival.

Finally, say in your mind, "May peace be mine. May peace be with my parents. May peace be with all beings." Take a few deep breaths. Relax with your eyes closed for a few more minutes, and when you feel like it, open your eyes.

Spousal Love

Attraction to and caring for another person are significant forces that exist to fulfill our adult biological and emotional needs. Throughout history, and especially in modern societies, sensual attraction and sexual fulfillment play important roles in maintaining marital love. In addition, each culture has set up rules, guidelines, and institutions to ensure that marriages are maintained in a socially harmonious and acceptable way.

However, marital relationships have been, and continue to be, a major cause of distress for many people. Divorce rates are going up, and many complaints and accusations are exchanged between spouses. When I visit some of my friends who have fallen in love, they talk as though they have finally found the ultimate bliss that they were searching for all their lives and could not find until now. Then, during a subsequent visit, I find the same people fallen, or falling, out of love. I see them acting as though the world has ended.

How is it possible that two people who were so delighted at the discovery of each other and thought it was the most wonderful thing that happened to them wind up spending the rest of their lives wishing it had never happened? How is it possible that love, the most important building block of human society, and perhaps of the species, ends up riding such a disastrous roller coaster? Is there anything we can learn from the ever-increasing number of marital breakups in order to gain some insight that will help us move toward a marital and family life where disharmony is the rare exception rather than the rule? Before we search for some answers, let us look at a typical marital drama.

CAN LOVE
TURN INTO HATE?

Several years ago, I visited a friend in Long Island, New York. He was a very handsome and smart businessman. He had just fallen in love with a woman. I was happy for him.

He talked constantly about her. It was the best thing that had ever happened to him, she was everything he wanted in a woman, and they decided to get married.

About a year after the wedding, I visited him again and learned that things had changed completely. The marriage had fallen apart and they had separated. He was very angry with her. He said, "She ruined my life. She is the worst thing that ever happened to me and I hate her." He went on and on, accusing and blaming her. After listening to him for a while, my first question to him was "What happened to your love?" The answer was "I don't love her anymore; I hate her." My next question was "Can love turn into hate?"

To understand the mechanics of such a situation, try to put yourself in either my friend's position or his wife's. As long as you were attracted to the other person and that person could fulfill your needs and expectations, you could accept the person. Maybe you call that acceptance the fulfillment of love. At some point in your relationship, one or both of you could not find fulfillment anymore, which started the chain reaction that led to losing interest in each other. Adding fuel to the fire, the resulting frustration turned into hatred and uncontrollable anger.

Maybe it was never genuine love to begin with. As is often the case, the sensual attraction was mistakenly equated with honest love. If the love was primarily genuine love, and only secondarily sensual love, it is most likely that the relationship would never have come to the crisis it did. If there was at least a fair component of genuine love, the two people could have departed as friends without hating each other, as happened in this case. This is possible only through mutual understanding and the realization that personality differences have made the continuation of the spousal relationship unworkable.

But what is genuine love?

GENUINE LOVE

Genuine love has many characteristics. Most important, there is a sincere interest in the happiness and well-being of the other person. When we say "I love you," if it is accompanied by this honest and heartfelt interest in the other's well-being, then it expresses genuine love. Obviously, in a relationship based on such love, hatred and the possibility of hurting the other person are totally nonexistent.

Second, there are no strings attached to the loving. No returns are expected, only an interest in the other person's happiness and well-being. Love is not an investment. Returns that do happen to come are accepted thankfully as a bonus and not as dues. There is no coercion on the other person to fulfill one's desires and expectations. The common formulas "You should love me because I love you" and "I did that for you, so you do this for me" are not present.

Third, in genuine love, self-reliance coexists with sharing.

Fourth, genuine love understands, with empathy and compassion, the human condition of the other person, particularly that person's mix of strengths and weaknesses. There is understanding of the uniqueness of the individual and the person's right to that uniqueness. This implies that, while there is the recognition that problems and difficulties exist, there is no blaming. Instead, there is joint action carried out in harmony to solve the problems. Genuine love will make it impossible to cause pain purposely to each other in the pursuit of solutions.

Finally, in the case of two people who have those qualities and who feel they can share their lives for even greater well-being and happiness, they will have the special, genuine love needed for a spousal relationship that will blossom and last.

So, the key building blocks of a loving and lasting relationship include absence of selfishness, the presence of caring, self-reliance coexisting with sharing, compassion and understanding, respect for the other's uniqueness, absence of blaming, and a genuine interest in the welfare of each other. If the relationship between my friend and his wife had been based on these conditions, then it is hard to imagine that it ever would have ended the way it did, causing pain and suffering to both.

As a final point on this subject, let us recognize that it is not love that can cause pain and hurt; rather, it is the absence of the characteristics we have just discussed. In other words, what causes pain and hurt is the lack of genuine love.

REFLECTION

If you believe that you have ever been hurt by love, this simple reflection will help you on the path to understanding and healing the hurts.

You don't necessarily have to come up with definitive answers to these questions. All that you are looking for here is to identify and develop greater awareness of factors that may hinder your relationships and cause hurt within you. That awareness will help you to work on difficult areas of love.

Have a friend read this to you, or tape it and play it back, or simply read through it first and then practice:

Close your eyes and relax, but maintain awareness of your thoughts. Now, go deep within yourself and try to connect with your hurt feelings. Let the feelings relating to your hurts flow freely out. When you connect with the energy of hurt, see whether you can recognize the cause of it.

Could it be that, being attached to the idea of "returns" in the relationship, you were expecting too much, and these expectations were not met? These could include lust or desires that were not satisfied. Maybe your disappointment, fear, anger, hate, or jealousy brought about this pain. Do you see any of these emotions contributing to and maintaining your hurt feelings?

Do you think you were too dependent on the other person? Do you think more self-reliance from each of you could ease things in the future? What does self-reliance mean to you? In the future, do you think that greater acceptance of individual differences would help to make this and other relationships better? Spend a few minutes on these thoughts.

Now, make a choice to let go of your attachment to the expectations or jealousy or anger, and be grateful for the experience just as it was. Let love into your heart. Let the hurts be replaced by the positive energy of love. Let your objective awareness and love shed some light on your mental state. Take a few deep breaths. When you are ready, open your eyes.

LOVE CAN NEVER
BREAK YOUR HEART

Love can bring you great comfort. Think of a moment when you were deeply, genuinely interested in the happiness of another person. How did you feel on such an occasion? A loving mother would know this feeling very well. If you could have the same feelings of love for another person that a loving mother has for her child, you would know it can bring you great comfort.

In pure love, anxiety is absent. Instead of emotional reaction, there is calm response. When I think of a situation or a person with the calmness of love, only wholesome thoughts and feelings arise in me. When I experience this soothing effect, I know the power of love can never harm me or others.

Let me share an example with you. When my mother died, I went through much pain. I fainted when I heard the news. I cried for days. I thought it was because I loved her. Later I realized that my love had been lost in the desire that my mother's life continue for my own comfort and warmth. I wouldn't say it is wrong to feel that way. But as I went deeper into my sadness I realized that my pain resulted from my selfish interest in her, rather than from my selfless relationship. This is a very fine line for a mind to understand.

I meditated every day to ease my pain. My mind began to get clearer, and my emotions settled. When the sadness and anxiety moved away, calm, pleasant feelings arose in me again. Now I could just smile with a pure feeling of love for her. I began to realize the conflict between my wish to see her alive and her own journey of life. She has the right to move on in her journey. Why should her death traumatize me? With love, I could wish her a happy journey. It was a comforting feeling. If love doesn't bring comfort, it is not love.

Experience of this pain caused by such inner turmoil is called heartbreak. The stronger the selfish attachment, the stronger the heartbreak will be. Intense emotions always have physical effects. When you experience anger, fear, or jealousy, you can feel them in your body.

In this society, many mistake selfish attachment as an essential characteristic of love. Because of this, we believe that it is love that "breaks" our hearts. Only selfishness can break the heart, because selfishness is the hook in conditional love. Unconditional love (*metta*) has no such hooks; therefore, it cannot break the heart. To get over a heartbreak, you need to find a way to let go of your selfish attachment. Strive to develop unconditional love to replace the selfish attachment that you might have mistaken for love. Let go of attachment and you will find love within you. Love can never break your heart. True love (*metta*) can only heal it.

Do You Want to
Be Loved?

One of my students who is a close friend once told me, "Bhante, I have been alone too long. Would you please pray for me? Pray for the right man to come to me. I know he is out there."

She described to me the type of man she was waiting for: a kind, caring person who would love her unconditionally and accept her for who she was. She said that he should be an unselfish, honest, and generous person. After listening to her for a while, I said to her that the best I could do was to pray, not for the appearance of that man, but for the discovery, and maybe cultivation, within herself of all the qualities she wanted in a man. I told her that once she experienced those qualities within herself, there would be plenty of good men who would be attracted to her.

I encouraged her to spend time looking within and working on herself, instead of waiting with anxiety and frustration for the ideal man. I said, "Maybe the wonderful man you are looking for is waiting for a wonderful woman. Are you ready now to fit into that spot? If not, are you prepared to do what is necessary so that you become the one qualified to fill the spot?"

I often meet people who are selfish, uncaring, unhappy, and aggressive. I see men who have a very poor image of women and women who are angry with men. They are looking for a relationship with someone who is unselfish, caring, happy, and gentle. They go on blaming others for their not being loved. If you believe that men are terrible, how are you going to attract a good man? If you believe women are detestable, how are you going to attract the right woman? What you don't believe is not going to be real to you.

We have a saying in Sri Lanka that a flower that is full of nectar does not have to beg the honeybees to pollinate it. The bees will know how to find the flower so long as it has nectar. Once they find the flower, they will also be very careful not to destroy it.

If you want to attract human "honeybees," you need to be a flower—not just a beautiful flower but one that also has nectar, a sweet essence. One may be a physically beautiful person, but if the inside is ugly and empty, one will attract only superficial attention. For the bees, the outside of a flower does not matter much, because they know the sweetness is in the essence. For human beings, spirituality and love constitute the nectar of life, the sweet essence within.

FROM ORDINARY LOVE TO UNCONDITIONAL LOVE

As mentioned before, what we ordinarily think of as love has a hidden but very powerful component of self-love (ego-love) that overshadows the love for others. In ordinary loving, we do not even realize that there is this all-powerful ego-love. And it is exactly the severe imbalance between this hidden ego-love and the love for others that causes us problems, difficulties, and, therefore, suffering. Note that loving oneself as a human being is healthy, should be nurtured, and is very different from ego-love, which inflates one's value of self at the expense of another human being.

Obviously, if the suffering is caused by the weight of the ego-love, we have to weaken or get rid of it and enhance our genuine love for others in our life and, better still, for all living beings. The next question is, how do we do that? One way it can be realized is through a very effective and time-tested Buddhist meditation technique called the cultivation of boundless selfless love (*metta bhavana*). This is also sometimes called loving-kindness meditation.

This universal-love meditation involves allowing feelings of love to gradually extend outward from oneself, to those in the same room, to those in one's home, community, and so forth, until this love encompasses the whole world, compassionately including even those who may have caused us pain.

Some beginning meditators may have difficulty with the concept of universal-love meditation, particularly the idea of extending love to those who may have hurt them. Remember that by extending compassionate love to those who may have caused us pain, the one to gain the greatest benefit—inner peace—is you.

In principle, we're using thought substitution, a practice also used in modern psychology. You substitute a wholesome thought for an unwholesome thought, and when this is practiced regularly over a reasonable length of time, the influence of the wholesome thought takes root, weakening or dislodging the other. Thus universal-love meditation helps to weaken the inflated ego-love and enhance our genuine love for all living beings including ourselves, thereby bringing us greater peace in daily living.

Let us try out a practical universal-love meditation based on the method we outlined.

UNIVERSAL-LOVE MEDITATION

Have a friend read this to you, tape it and play it back for yourself, or simply read through it and then practice it:

Sit comfortably, making sure your back is straight, and gently close your eyes. Remind yourself that you have chosen these few minutes to lead yourself into a loving state. Any distracting thoughts can wait until you finish this meditation.

Take a few deep breaths and become centered. Feel your whole body with your mind. Feel close to yourself. Try to touch yourself with your mind, respectfully and lovingly. Say to yourself, "I love myself and I love my whole being." Pay attention to every word; feel a direct connection to them. Let loving thoughts come from the center of your heart and let them move through your whole being. You can even visualize this symbolically. Keep repeating to yourself, "I love myself and I love my whole being" for a few minutes and feel a harmonious relationship with yourself. Stay with this thought until you can feel it having a positive effect.

Now, look at yourself objectively. You are the observer and, at the same time, you are the observed. The observer is the mother and the observed is the child. Feel motherly love toward yourself. Spend a few minutes wishing yourself well. Think clearly, "May I be well, happy, and peaceful." Pay undivided attention to each word and connect fully with its meaning. Feel that you are blessing yourself with your own loving thoughts. Take a minute or two for this.

Now is the time for you to share this experience with others. You choose to connect with those you know and those you don't know with the same loving, caring, and compassionate thoughts. Again remind yourself that this is no time for any negative thoughts or past memories. If past memories sneak in and begin to bother you, gently put them aside.

Begin with your parents. Think, "May my parents be well, happy, and peaceful." Repeat this a few times. Try to remain connected to them with the warmth of your love and caring.

Now expand your love to other members of your immediate and extended family. Think, "May my children, brothers, sisters, and grandparents be well, happy, and peaceful." Repeat this a few times. Try to remain connected to them with genuine love for them.

Next think, "May my other relatives, friends, and neighbors be well, happy, and peaceful." See all of them walk into a circle of love in your heart. Repeat this a few times.

Now, with compassion, think of those who may have caused you pain, and extend unconditional love to them. In your mind, repeat a few times, "May those who caused hurt in the past be well."

Next, think of all human beings as one family, the human family, and wish them well, wish them peace. "May all human beings be well, happy, and peaceful." Repeat this a few times.

Finally, expand your love to all living beings. "May all living beings be well, happy, and peaceful." Think of all life, all conscious living beings. Take this moment to connect to them with only positive, loving thoughts.

Slowly bring your attention to your breath. Spend a few minutes focusing on your breath. Then, when you feel ready, gently open your eyes.

CHAPTER FIVE

Meditation and the Reflective Mind

A mind not to be changed by place or time;
The mind is its own place,
And in itself
Can make a heav'n of hell,
A hell of heav'n.

JOHN MILTON, *Paradise Lost*

ASK YOURSELF

In order to prepare for what we are going to explore in this chapter, let us start by asking ourselves some questions. As before, there are no right or wrong answers. You might want to write down the answers that come to mind.

Do you think that your mind is too active or that it gets distracted easily? Do you feel that your life is stressful? Do you often wish you were able to slow down and relax, but cannot? Like many people, do you have a tendency to lose control easily and explode with emotions such as anger?

Have you been concerned at any time that your health was being affected by mental stress and a rushed lifestyle? Do you think you need to make changes in your life to find more inner peace and fulfillment? How often have you tried meditation or relaxation exercises? If you have tried them, have you experienced any benefits?

As you may know, your quality of life depends greatly on the state of your mind. How often do you take time to observe what is going on in your mind? What kind of exercises could you do to know your mind and thoughts better and to have more control over them?

Meditation means many things to many people. How familiar are you with it? What are your views on the many effects of meditation? Do you view it mainly as empowerment to perform psychic feats? A means to relaxation? A technique for attaining highs similar to those provided by drugs? Or a way to the attainment of permanent peace?

Do you think that the human mind would yield to change? In a larger context, do you think you can shape your destiny?

Now that your mind is stimulated, let us move on.

THE JIGSAW PUZZLE

A teacher was trying to convey an important point about world peace to his young students: If they really cared and wanted to do something about it, they needed to begin with themselves. Although the children had a natural desire for peace, they could not see how one person's becoming peaceful could make a difference to world peace. After all, to them the world was an enormous and overwhelming place and they were insignificant specks in it.

The teacher attempted to answer their disbelief in many ways, but no explanation convinced them. The teacher was frustrated with his inability to convince his students, and he spent his evening at home preoccupied with the challenge.

The next morning, the teacher arrived at the classroom smiling and looking very confident. He had brought with him a jigsaw puzzle that, when put together, showed a man on one side and a map of the world on the other. He scattered the pieces for the world map and asked the children to assemble them. At first the children were enthusiastic, but soon they became discouraged because the task was very difficult.

The teacher watched the children struggle for a few minutes and then told them to stop. "Let me show you an easy way to put the world together," the teacher said, and asked the students to turn the puzzle over and to assemble the picture of the man. Effortlessly and with enthusiasm the students put the picture of the man together because they could easily recognize body parts such as eyes, legs, and arms. When they were finished, the teacher asked the students to turn the picture over. Sure enough, there was a perfect puzzle world on the other side.

"See," the teacher said, "it is far easier to put the person together than the entire world. In our world, when the human being becomes perfect, the world will naturally become perfect."

Explaining the lesson intended by his jigsaw puzzle, he

continued, "If we want a peaceful world, we need to have peaceful individuals in it, because the world is made of individuals. When the minds of individual human beings are violent, there is violence in the world. Our schools, cities, countries, and world are nothing but a collection of individuals. Without peace in the minds and hearts of the people, there will be no peace in the world. If you are really interested in world peace, the most valuable contribution you can make to achieve it is to work hard toward peace within yourself, and to encourage others within your influence to do the same. Then you can proudly call yourself a peacemaker of the world."

CALMING THE MIND

Meditation is a journey one takes to reach peace. It is the vehicle, but not the destination. Although the final destination is peace, the journey is a rewarding experience for personal growth, self-discovery, and healing of one's heart.

Formal meditation necessitates sitting still and allowing one's mind to be restful. When we are physically tired, we rest in order to energize the body in preparation for the next physical activity. If we don't get proper rest, not only will we be deprived of optimal energy for physical activities, but we also risk becoming sick.

What we don't usually realize is that, just like the body, the mind also needs rest if it is to perform its tasks effectively. The mind is like a machine that never stops working. During sleep, it slows down but still does not stop. For the mind to rest and calm down, it has to be deliberately but gently trained; otherwise it keeps working at lightning speed, with penalties to be paid in the form of sickness.

It is extremely important to become aware of the needs of our mind and pay serious attention to our mental well-being. A sound, clear, and rested mind is essential if we are to fully enjoy the many blessings that life offers us. Such a tranquil mind can be realized through meditation. With meditation, we can help the mind to calm down and get a good rest. The calm mind can uncover and reawaken unused resources within us.

"Mind-Sitting"

One of my early teachers calls sitting meditation "mind-sitting," likening it to baby-sitting. It involves observing, paying attention, and taking care. In addition, it requires sitting alone and still. Thus, meditation trains the mind to "sit." Sitting is an essential practice for spiritual progress. It is through sitting in meditation that many have attained peace and enlightenment.

With the sitting posture, the body can make the optimum contribution toward achieving a calm mind. Some claim that sitting cross-legged is the only way they can meditate. Sitting meditation seems to be especially effective in helping one to reach higher mental states. Yet sitting is not the only way to meditate. Buddhist meditation teachers usually teach four different postures for meditation— sitting, walking, standing, and lying down.

Posture

When you practice sitting meditation, the way you sit—your posture—often affects the quality of awareness. Sit with your back as erect as possible and draw the chin in slightly. Keep your palms on your lap with the right palm on the left. Sitting in this way helps you to stay alert. Breathing should always be normal, that is, not forced.

If you are a beginner, I suggest you try different ways to sit in order to find the most comfortable position for yourself. Initially, you could use a pillow, bench, cushion, or just a mat on the floor to sit on. Try different positions. While sitting cross-legged is the position favored by most meditators, it is very important to choose a position that is comfortable for you, one you can maintain for the duration of the meditation. At the same time, it must be a position that keeps you alert and does not lull you into drowsiness or sleep.

In the beginning, you might feel some discomfort with your position. Be patient until you get used to it. By all means change your posture if it becomes unbearable while meditating. Do it mindfully and patiently.

Place

To help your mind to focus and your body to relax, choose a quiet place for your meditation. If you meditate regularly, set up a special place in your house and create a pleasant environment. It could be just a corner of a room, or if you have an extra room, it would be wonderful to have it devoted to meditation. Many of my students have created such special spaces for sitting. Keep it simple and make it pleasant.

Time

What is the best time to meditate? Although any time is a good time, find the most suitable time for yourself, taking into consideration your habits, commitments, and lifestyle. The time when you are least distracted but alert is the ideal time for meditation.

For me, I have found the perfect time for meditation to be immediately after waking. Upon awakening, I feel rested and mentally less distracted. After having a few hours of rest from sensory stimulation, the brain usually works at a slower pace, which helps with the meditation. Another advantage to meditating first thing in the morning is that it is usually easier to spare fifteen or twenty minutes before other activities begin to compete for your time. All these factors can help you to get the mind focused and to concentrate better. If you are not a morning person, or if you need coffee to wake up, then the morning may not be the best time for you.

In the temple where I lived as a novice monk, we woke up at four-thirty every morning. By five, we were all sitting in the meditation room. That early morning routine has instilled in me a habit of sitting on my bed and meditating as soon as I wake up. I find it a wonderful way to start the day.

The other most convenient time for me is when I retire

to bed. Just before lying down, I sit for ten or fifteen minutes. Ending the day by reflecting on the day's events and having a few moments of peace with myself helps me to sleep better.

Distractions

There are distracting sounds and noises around us most of the time. When you sit to meditate, the fewer external distractions you have, the easier it will be for you to get into a calm state. But it is not possible for most of us to find a place completely free of noise. Actually, when you meditate, nothing is supposed to be considered a "distraction," unless it's unbearable. If the sounds are unbearable, you must do something about them. Otherwise, learn to allow any experience of the moment to be part of your meditation.

As you learn to be an observer of all experience in its true nature, noises and sounds will not distract you anymore. It is not the sounds that you have to worry about, but what the mind does with the experience of sounds. Let the sounds come and go and watch how your mind reacts to them. Mastery of that aspect of meditation is a major step forward in your spiritual growth.

HEALING FOR STRESS

In modern society, we lead very rushed lives. Such a lifestyle results in stress and can cause many mental and physical problems. Studies have shown that 70 to 80 percent of all diseases and illnesses of the body and mind are related to stress.

Stress is caused by attitude and lifestyle, rather than by workload or life's challenges. More and more health professionals are beginning to understand and admit the importance of learning to relax the body and mind for stress management. The West has only recently begun to discover the healing effects of meditation, which has been a well-established practice in the East for thousands of years.

Tranquility meditation (*samatha bhavana*) is a very effective tool for bringing one's mental energy into focus. For the beginner, the purpose of meditation is to bring the mind into a restful and relaxed state. Meditation can heal the body and mind, and it can be a preventive tool. If you begin the day with restful meditation, the peace you experience will help you to calmly face the challenges of the day.

While we sleep, the body may be resting but the mind can be as active as when we're awake. That is why we cannot assume that the mind gets its proper rest while we are sleeping. We need to lead the mind into a restful state while we are consciously awake. The Buddhist techniques of meditation can help bring the mind into this state of restfulness. That is the only way we can provide extra care for the mind so that it can return with a full charge of mental energy. I have found the benefits from meditation in my own life to be phenomenal.

I lead a very busy life. First, there are my travels to many parts of the world. Sometimes I travel more than a hundred thousand miles in a year. When I am back home in

North America, there are endless teaching and counseling sessions, and all the unavoidable mundane tasks that need attention in order to keep things moving. I would say that my schedule is an extremely busy one by any standard, and certainly quite unusual for a Buddhist monk.

My friends are amazed at how much I accomplish. I have often been asked how I manage to do all this and still show no signs of stress, maintain my peace of mind, and live a happy life. My answer is simple: meditation. I begin each day with meditation, and no matter how busy the day becomes, I end the day with meditation. During the evening session, I lead my mind into a relaxed and peaceful state that I call my inner sanctuary, where I let go of the day's concerns. My meditative practice helps me to be as busy as I want during the day but still be unaffected by forces around me. I am aware that it is my own attitudes, beliefs, feelings, and thoughts that create stress in me, not what is out in the world. This enhances the effectiveness of my daily meditation.

BREATH CONSCIOUSNESS MEDITATION

Let us try a simple exercise in the awareness of breathing, a meditation called *anapana sati*. The object of this is to refresh the mind, eliminate stress, and experience inner peace.

It doesn't matter where you are. You could be in your office, in your home, sitting in a bus, or formally sitting on a meditation cushion. While it may be practiced at any time of the day, it is most needed when you feel stressed and distracted mentally.

Make sure you are physically comfortable. Close your eyes. Take a few deep breaths. As you breathe in, hold the breath briefly. As you breathe out, slowly release the breath, making sure you are emptying the maximum possible amount of air each time. Note that this enhanced breathing is done only at the beginning to relax yourself; in actual meditation, one does not force any changes on one's natural breathing.

Now, begin to breathe normally. Pay attention to the movement of your natural breath. Try to feel the sensation of your breath in the inner lining of your nostrils. For now, think of the breath as the only thing that exists in the world. Nothing else matters at this moment. Pay attention to each breath and follow its movement.

Gradually build up full focus on your breath. As you breathe in, experience peace with your breath. As you breathe out, let go of your concerns and bodily tensions.

Free yourself from the last moment and free yourself from the next moment. Let your mind flow with the rhythm of your breath and be in this present moment.

You might find distracting thoughts in your mind, particularly at the beginning of your meditation. Don't try to push them away or struggle with them. When you are reading an interesting book, sometimes your attention is so focused that you may not hear or see what happens around you. Likewise, as your attention on breathing deepens, you will not be distracted by what is going on around you. Be in touch with the present moment; try to focus your attention fully on your breath. Let the distractions come and go on their own. As your mind begins to wander, slowly bring your attention back to your breathing.

Be with your breathing for as long as you wish. Be fully focused on your breathing. Let each breath refresh your mind and relax your body. When you have rested for a while, open your eyes slowly.

PEACE WILL COME

In the Buddhist temple in Sri Lanka where I started my life as a young monk, we used the Pali word *sati* in referring to meditation. Practicing *sati* is practicing to be wakeful and attentive to the inner world of experience. It is also a way to be still and quiet within oneself. The senior monks told me that when I sit to meditate, I should have no expectations of results. This is because learning to meditate is learning to be free of expectations altogether. It is only when your mind is free of all expectations that real peace begins to sprout within it.

All of these instructions and explanations baffled me at the time, because even though I was in monk's clothes, I was a boy in my early teens. How could I sit still, expecting nothing? An impossible task! Although I did not know how to meditate properly at the time, even meditation incorrectly done was hard work. And I thought that nothing was wrong with expecting results—at least peacefulness—from my hard work. Later on in my practice, I realized how expectations could cause anxiety and interfere with the progress of inner stillness. Then I was able to understand the importance of freeing my mind from expectations at the time of meditation.

Like most beginners, I was fighting my thoughts, expecting them to go away. I thought that if I could chase my thoughts away, I would be able to experience peace. It took me years before I completely understood why it was not possible to establish *sati* without freeing the mind from expectations. Expectations meant that I was clinging to something of the future, and they were the reason I could not be peaceful.

The correct method to establish *sati* is to be fully in harmony with the present moment. It is to be fully awake to what arises and passes through the mind, without fighting it. This brings about peace within.

To bring peace to the world, the individual has to have peace within himself or herself. The peaceful person brings joy to himself or herself as well as to others and to the world at large. Meditation is a means of regaining one's lost mental equilibrium and achieving inner and outer peace.

The confused person, one who is angry or violent, mentally scattered, or aggressive, brings suffering to himself or herself and to the world. A person of peace causes no harm to self or to others; rather, he or she becomes a peacemaker. If each of us moves in the direction of developing inner peace through the process of meditation, we bring harmony not only to ourselves but also to the whole world. Consequently, what may at first appear to be a selfish act is actually one that effectively brings about universal peace and happiness by eliminating one's own suffering as well as the suffering of the world.

When I was young, if a meditation teacher said, "Peace will come," I would ask, "When?" To me, it seemed like a fair question. Later on, as I began to understand things, I realized that you cannot create peace by force or by dwelling on expectations. The most difficult lesson for a novice meditator is developing patience. Peace has to come on its own. The process is similar to the blossoming of a flower.

If you want a flower to blossom, you cannot force it. Let's say that you have a rosebush in your garden. You faithfully devote your time to watering it and protecting it from insects. As the plant grows, you become impatient to see the flowers. When the buds appear, you still need to devote time to its care. Finally a flower blooms, and at last you can enjoy its fragrance and beauty.

Cultivating patience is an important virtue. Patience will keep your mind free of expectations until it is time for the "flower" of peace to blossom. In the meantime, when you sit to meditate, stop wishing and expecting. Pay attention to the present moment and let the moments unfold as life moves on. Then peace will come.

TAMING THE "CRAZY MIND"

It was the second day of a meditation retreat I was leading. One older gentleman who was not very comfortable with the idea of meditation had come to the retreat primarily to please his wife. He was not confident that he would survive two days of meditation. Yet he decided to see if meditation could bring him peace. I noticed the first day that he tried very hard to be a good student. When the second day arrived, however, he was ready to leave the retreat and go home. He came hoping to find peace, but instead he was more frustrated than when he began.

He said, "I don't think I can meditate. I am one of those people with an active mind. When I try to meditate, my mind goes crazy and I can't stop it." His complaint is a familiar one to those just beginning to meditate.

I told him, "I am fully aware of what you are experiencing. It is a normal phase that beginning meditators go through. Your mind does not go crazy as a result of trying to meditate. When you begin to meditate, you become aware of the 'craziness' in your mind, maybe for the first time. Some people are so surprised by what they discover when they first begin to meditate. Seeing the inner chaos, they ask, 'Is that me? Is that my mind?' This very awareness of the incessantly wandering mind is in fact the first milestone of progress on the meditative path."

Every beginning meditator should recognize the busy, fast-running, and often erratic nature of the human mind as the first lesson of meditation. The meditator's first major challenge is to watch the "crazy mind" patiently, learn what the untrained mind is like, and not run away from unfamiliar distractions. If you keep practicing meditation, you will not call it the "crazy mind" anymore. You will be able to accept the craziness as the mind's normal nature, and, going a step further, you will learn how to tame the mind and keep it calm and tranquil always. When the "crazy mind" begins to slow down, you will be taking just the first steps of a long journey toward self-discovery and self-understanding.

The human mind is very complex. The Buddha, describing the nature of the mind, said, "It is difficult to control, elusive, and inclines toward pleasure. Taming the mind is good. A tamed mind brings happiness." When you begin to meditate, you will notice that your thoughts race at a tremendous speed. For those who are not used to paying close attention to their minds, meditation can be a disturbing experience. It will be disturbing to hear the "noise" in your mind, to which you have never previously opened your ears. In reality, meditation does not bring you any new disturbance; it just makes noticeable what is already there.

When you meditate, you listen to your mind because the only way you can understand yourself better is to understand what is going on in your mind. Observe your thoughts carefully.

The quality of your life depends largely on the state of your mind. An unstable, fluctuating mind can make life feel like a heavy burden. Wakefulness lightens the mind and helps you to become aware of the forces of the mind and to direct them where you wish. Negative emotions such as depression, tension, and anxiety can limit your natural potential and retard your progress on the path to happiness. Such inner turmoil is a result of unnoticed, unattended, and neglected thoughts and feelings. They need to be filtered through the eye of wakefulness.

Sit still without trying to run away from the "crazy mind." Learn to pay attention to the activities of your mind.

They are part of what makes you who you are. You will discover that initially it is very difficult to maintain your awareness for more than a few minutes. That is another important discovery on the meditative path.

CALMING THE MIND

Find a place where you can sit for a while without many distractions. Sit comfortably with your back straight. You may sit on a meditation pillow, a cushion, or a chair. If you have any difficulty with your back, sit against the wall. Gently rest your hands on your lap. Keep your shoulders loose and your entire body relaxed. Close your eyes.

Pay attention to your breathing. Begin to count each breath as you inhale and exhale. Breathing in is count one, breathing out is count two, breathing in is count three, and so on. Just be mindful of your breath as you inhale and exhale. When you have counted up to ten, go back to one again and repeat the process. Keep on counting until you can get your mind fully focused on your breath. Then stop counting so that you can concentrate fully on just the breath, to the exclusion of everything else.

Allow your breathing to conform to its natural rhythm. Do not try to control it in any way.

Now introduce a slight enhancement to help you focus on the breath even better. As you breathe mindfully, notice the beginning, the middle, and the end of each breath. When you inhale, feel the beginning of the breath in the tip of your nostrils, the middle of the breath in your chest, and the end in your abdomen. As you exhale, feel the beginning of the breath in the abdomen, the middle in your chest area, and the end in your nostrils.

At times, you may experience physical discomfort or different sensations in your body. When that happens, you can mindfully breathe into that area and relax. Or you can take your mind away from the breath, pay attention to your body, and make any necessary adjustments, then slowly come back to your breath again.

From time to time, you will notice distractions in your mind. Wandering thoughts or feelings will disturb your attention. Each time a distracting thought appears, simply acknowledge it, let it disappear on its own, and gently bring your focus back to the breath. If your mind becomes too restless or begins to wander into too many distracting thoughts, take a few deep breaths. Hold each breath for a few seconds and slowly release it, letting your thoughts go with your breath. Come back to your breathing when your thoughts settle down. Continue to breathe naturally, and let your mind slow down into the rhythm of the breath.

Allow yourself at least fifteen to twenty minutes to meditate. That is how long it normally takes to have a calming experience. If you can, sit longer. Before opening your eyes, appreciate the blessings of life and of everything in life.

Then gently get up and set about your normal business of the day. In order to carry the benefits of this meditative experience into the day, try not to rush into things. Instead,

for at least an hour or two immediately following the meditation, try to keep the same level of gentleness that you
maintained during the meditation.

AWAKENING

It is with the practice of introspective awareness that we can
find our way back to our inner center. Once a curious seeker
asked the Buddha, "Venerable sir, what are you?" The Buddha simply said, "I am the awake." This is an unusual way to
define oneself. If he gave you the same answer, you might say,
"Me too, venerable sir." After all, you are not sleeping, which
is why you're able to talk to the Buddha. But the wakefulness
the Buddha was talking about didn't mean not being asleep.
The Buddha meant that even when we think we're awake, if
we are not in touch with reality, if we don't see things as they
really are, then conscious awareness is absent.

In normal waking hours, much of the time our mind
dwells on the past and on the future. But the past and the
future are not reality. Think on that deeply for a moment.
The past and the future don't really exist. Only the present is
reality. As long as our minds are in the past or in the future,
in an absolute sense we are dreaming. To dream is to keep
your mind occupied with something that doesn't exist.

In drifting away to the past or worrying about what
happened before, the mind wanders in dreams. In drifting
away to the future, anxious or fearful of what is to come,
the mind also wanders in dreams. With these dreams we

experience disappointment, anger, fear, jealousy, pleasure, pain, or many other feelings.

Some of us are so addicted to the world of fantasy that we live there most of the time—and therefore suffer most of the time. Observe your thoughts for a while to see how many of them are related to the past and future and how many to the present moment. In doing so, you will make an amazing discovery about your normal existence, and you will come to a very profound realization.

The whole purpose of Buddhist meditation is to avoid hypnotic trance, fantasy, or imaginary journeys. The Buddhist approach to meditation begins with the understanding that we are *already hypnotized*. Most of the thoughts and ideas in the unenlightened mind are not the result of conscious, objective discernment, but are the product of many, many unconscious hypnotic suggestions accumulated through years of social and cultural conditioning. Introspective meditation begins a process that helps dehypnotize and decondition the mind and prepare it for the *summum bonum*, or highest good, of enlightenment.

The way out of suffering requires training ourselves to live in the present. The central theme of introspective meditation is simply to live in the present moment. It is not easy to understand that living in the dream world of the past and the future is a waste of one's precious life. The dreams of the past and future are like layers of clouds that block the sunlight from reaching us. In Buddhist terms, the mind's habitual dwelling in the past and future keeps us from experiencing wisdom, happiness, and peace.

Let us listen every day to the echo of the Buddha's teaching: "Awaken! Awaken! Awaken!"

BREATH, THE LIFE FORCE

In our mostly unnoticed but incessantly and quietly active breath, the Buddha discovered an important aid to spiritual awakening. We were born breathing and continue to breathe till we die. This most dependable and always accessible breath holds the golden key to peace, happiness, and enlightenment. Anchor yourself to your breath, deepen self-awareness through mindfulness practice, and you will master your mind. Then peace and happiness will not leave you.

Yogis in India hold the belief that the breath can assist them in unlocking psychic powers and achieving spiritual transcendence. In recognition of that, they practice different types of breathing meditations, called *pranayama* meditations. In Sanskrit, *prana* means "life force," an acknowledgment that the breath holds one's power of life; it is the tangible indicator that we are alive. The difference between yogic *pranayama* meditations and Buddhist meditations is that in *pranayama*, effort is applied beyond the involuntary action of breathing, whereas in Buddhist meditation no such effort is applied.

The mind and breathing are very much interlinked. Via our lungs, heart, and blood circulation, the oxygen we breathe finds its way to the building blocks of our life, the cells, to keep us alive. Our thoughts and emotions, which are the nontangible manifestations of the physical body, are closely connected with our breathing. So, we may say that the life force and the mind force are closely linked. Then it is not difficult to understand that a calming breath can be related to a calm mind.

We also know that the mind can affect the body. It is common knowledge that when we display very strong emotional reactions, such as rage or phobic fears, physical (bodily) reactions ensue. Common, noticeable physical manifestations are sweating, increased heart rate, and changes in breathing.

The breath is intimately connected with our feelings and emotions. Have you noticed how deep that connection is? When your emotions change from fear to excitement and from joy to peace, have you observed how your breath also changes? The breath moves in harmony with emotions, one way or the other.

When you are upset, sad, or angry, how often have you heard the advice "Sit down, take a deep breath, and relax"? In such moments, deep, controlled breaths will help you to calm the mind, which in turn will help you to relax the body. By paying attention to your breathing and consciously regulating it, you can initiate a healthy cycle of mind-body reactions that will help to heal both mind and body.

WHY MEDITATE ON BREATH?

The breath has a perfect natural rhythm, while our mind tends to naturally wander. When we try to anchor our mind to the breath, we find that it often slips. No wonder! The final lesson that the peaceful, gentle, and rhythmic breath teaches us is that the mind moves about like a mad monkey jumping from tree to tree. Thus we recognize the great disparity between breath and mind with regard to calmness. That awareness is the first step in our determination to bring the "mad monkey" to order with meditation.

The breath is a tool for the beginner as well as the advanced practitioner. I am a devoted and regular meditator on breathing, and it has given me great benefits. I know how the practice of mindfulness on breathing can help one to find self-confidence and inner strength. The breath can lead one from the initial accomplishment of simply calming the mind to a gradually deeper awareness and spiritual awakening.

When you start to experience the benefits of meditation on breathing, you begin to realize what a wonderful and helpful companion the breath is.

The Crab in the Puddle

I am sitting on a rock by a river, feeling very peaceful. Among the rocks there is a large puddle of water. The water is crystal clear and I can see very tiny fish moving in it. I can clearly see small stones and some leaves at the bottom as well.

Suddenly a crab, threatened by a predator, comes running from the riverbank and jumps into the puddle. As it dives to the bottom the puddle of water turns murky due to the agitation of the mud and dirt at the bottom. The crab is now invisible. So are the stones, leaves, and fish. Keeping my eyes focused on the puddle and the goings-on therein, I notice how the dirt is slowly settling to the river bottom. After some time, the water becomes clear again. All the objects can be seen as before. The crab is quietly enjoying its hard-won rest in its haven beneath the mud at the bottom of the river.

As I get up to leave the river, it occurs to me what a great lesson was contained in what I just witnessed. I feel like I am coming out of a classroom. Back home, the lesson becomes apparent as I try to meditate. After a few minutes of meditation, my mind is still and clear, like the puddle. There are no distractions. I feel peaceful. Yet, at any moment, extraneous thoughts can intrude, cloud the mind, and take away the stillness and clarity.

Whenever I meditate and my mind gets caught up in distractions, I think of the crab and the puddle, because what is happening in my mind is very similar to what happened to the puddle. The puddle of water is the mind, the crab is a distracting thought (triggered by sensory stimulation), the murkiness is the emotional agitation caused in the mind, and the objects at the bottom of the puddle are truths.

When the water is disturbed, the more mud and dirt there is at the bottom of the puddle, the murkier and darker the water will be. When the bottom is clean and free of dirt, it does not matter how much the puddle is agitated, for the water will always stay clean. An impoverished and confused mind is like a puddle with a lot of dirt and mud. Even a slight sensual distraction could stir up the emotions, and the mind could get murky.

In insight meditation, every time the dirt (in this case, the emotional agitation) surfaces, we try to filter it out with awareness. Awareness can go even deeper into the bottom, picking up dirt and filtering it out like the suction cleaner of a swimming pool. That is what should happen in a good meditation session.

The little crab in the puddle taught me a very simple but valuable lesson about the nature of my mind and meditation. Another realization it provides is that the simple things of nature, abundant everywhere, can teach me the important lessons I need to learn about life, if only I care to keep my eyes and ears open.

WALKING MEDITATION

Walking is a daily activity that we perform without thinking very much. Ordinarily, we don't see much significance in walking other than to get from one place to another. In meditation, walking is used as a tool for developing self-awareness. In the beginning, we practice a special way of walking to train the mind to be present. Eventually we will develop an ability to integrate walking in daily life as a simple tool of mindfulness practice. In practicing formal walking meditation, we do not walk to get anywhere, but to train the mind to be fully present during the action.

As you practice walking meditation, the movement of your body, the physical sensation of walking, and the awareness of this movement and sensation put you directly in touch with your body. I have noticed that those who have a poor image of, or dislike for, their body have greater difficulty doing walking practice. It may bring out deep feelings that you have about your body. I suggest that you be aware of whatever feelings arise as you do walking meditation. You may learn a few things about the nature of the relationship you have with your body.

If you intend to meditate for longer periods, you should alternate walking and sitting. When you feel that you have been sitting too long and are getting uncomfortable, you can continue to meditate by changing from sitting to walking.

One of my students practices walking meditation in his office for a few minutes behind closed doors to relieve tension during a stressful day. He said that when he is too restless to sit, walking meditation really helps him to relax and feel restful. You also can try this in your office (or elsewhere) any time of day and see how it helps you.

Find a comfortable place where you can walk about fifteen or twenty feet. It could be in your bedroom, living room, or outside. There should be two clearly recognizable objects to mark the beginning and end of the walking path, so that you will not have to count steps when walking.

Stand at one end of the walking path, close your eyes, and take a couple of deep breaths. As you release the breath relax the body and feel its presence.

Spend a couple of minutes tuning into your body. Stay aware of the whole body. Bring your attention to your feet. Feel the weight of your body on your feet. Open your eyes.

Clasp your hands in a relaxed manner in front of, or behind, your body. Begin to walk slowly, gazing at an imaginary point about five feet away so that your neck will be held in a comfortable position. Your eyes should not be focused on any object in particular. Pay attention to the movement of your feet. Be mindful of each foot as you lift it, move it forward, and place it on the ground.

If you walk too quickly or too slowly, it will be difficult for the mind to follow your steps. Find the speed that is most comfortable for you.

At the end of the path, stay still for the duration of about two breaths, then turn back mindfully. Now walk in this direction until you reach the beginning point. Close your eyes and pay attention to your body again for the duration of about four breaths. Open your eyes, mindfully turn, and continue the process.

A good duration for walking meditation is fifteen to twenty minutes.

Handle disturbing thoughts exactly as you did in the sitting meditation, that is, with gentle acknowledgment, allowing them to disappear on their own. Then patiently bring your attention back to your feet.

When you have come to the end of the walking meditation session, try to sit for a few minutes. I find that this helps me to live in the calmness achieved and to go deeper into the experience of peace.

INVITING SILENCE

I often meditate on this poem I wrote about silence. It helps me remember that silence does not mean emptiness.

I become the detached observer
And watch
My thoughts, with lives of their own
Flash and flutter
Rise and fall
Come and go
So many butterflies outside my window

And I smile
And I slow
My thoughts
To rest.
Patiently I calm them all
And come to rest.

Motionless, effortless, all quiet.
A great and peaceful ocean
Home to mysteries and treasure
At voiceless rest beneath the sea

With silent contemplation
And inner awareness
The mind clears its way
I enter the vastness

And drift beneath its gentle surface
In slow strong currents of a deeper life
Currents of serenity
Currents of love
Currents of joy
Currents of bliss

I am suddenly free
Free from a noisy mind
Free from a warring brain
Free to embrace the beauty of all life
Free to connect
With my inner essence
To know only peace and kindness
Love and joy
A moment of eternal freedom

Liberated by mind
The deepest part of me
Emerges from within
And with the small and subtle gentle touches
Silence speaks to me.

CHAPTER SIX

Death: From Foe to Friend

As to your life,
I reckon you are the leavings of many deaths;
No doubt I have died myself,
a thousand times before.

WALT WHITMAN

⟐ ASK YOURSELF ⟐

The journey of our life begins with birth and ends with death. The time of your death, the last beat of your heart, will always remain unknown to you. For some there is nothing more terrifying than facing that mysterious moment. You may fear death because it takes away everything, everything that you own or call your own, including your body. You will take nothing with you as you depart for an unknown destiny. But fearing death is not facing death honorably. It is important to remind ourselves from time to time of our final days in this life and to reflect on it in a positive way. How often do you take time to remind yourself that this mysterious moment is waiting for you? What kinds of thoughts, feelings, or emotions do you have as you deeply reflect on your own death?

I have spoken to hundreds of people who have been shattered, shaken, and utterly surprised by the unexpected news of a life-threatening accident or terminal illness. I have seen how the news of death casts dark shadows over lives and how people become angry, afraid, and miserable. When I see such people I realize how important it is for me to ask myself "How can I prepare myself to view my own death with peace, acceptance, fearlessness, and love? How can I prepare myself so that such news will not come to me as an unexpected surprise?"

And how about death of your loved ones? When you know somebody who dies, somebody who is close to you and whom you love and care for, it saddens you and causes great pain and suffering. Why does death cause us so much inner turmoil, confusion, and suffering? Can you see any healthier perspective or calmer reaction that might be in harmony with nature's way and that might help you to cope with a loved one's death without inflicting unnecessary pain and suffering?

THE FINISH LINE

Death is an inescapable fact of living. Sooner or later, all that is born has to succumb; death plays no favorites. Death is our common bond. Those whom we have cared for and loved leave the greatest void when they die. The deaths of our family members, our friends, and even our pets—some as dear to us as a best friend—have the greatest impact on us. Someone we can touch, feel, and speak with today can suddenly disappear into nothingness tomorrow.

Although death is commonplace, most of the time we fail to accept (or refuse to admit) that we are also steadily approaching it. Seldom does the thought occur that it could happen to us. And our denial extends to encompass others as well. So, when news arrives that someone we know has left this world—unless from a terminal illness or old age—it is often greeted with shock and surprise.

We have never been taught to accept the inevitability of death with emotional equanimity. We are not taught to be mindful of the undeniable fact that the finishing point of this great marathon called life, which started at birth, is death. Can we accept the sunrise but pretend that the sunset doesn't exist? Because of the artificially created fear of this natural and inevitable event, we keep thoughts of our own death and those of our loved ones at bay. No wonder we're so off guard when the news arrives about someone's death. Why do human beings imagine death to be the most fearsome thing in the universe and keep all thoughts of it sheltered away in the bunkers of our minds? I would like to suggest that it's because of our futile wish to be immortal, which comes from not understanding the phenomenon of death.

BLESS THEM WITH PEACE

As one of my functions as a monk, I make regular visits to dying people. In Sri Lanka, when people are dying, their relatives or friends will usually invite the monks to recite special teachings from Buddhist scriptures. Since the scriptures are the teachings of an enlightened person, they are words of wisdom that bring peace. Even if the person to whom we chant is not fully conscious, we believe that the words we recite can benefit the dying individual by producing a peaceful state of mind before death.

It is very common for Buddhists to sit by the deathbed and chant scriptures for this reason. Creating an atmosphere of peace around the person is very important. Even when sensory connections with the world are not fully functional, Buddhists believe the dying can feel the presence of people around them and can hear words and sounds. Many of those who have had near-death experiences have described being able to hear, see, and feel everything around them even though they were declared clinically dead.

Think of this for a moment. Suppose you are dying. As you are preparing for your final exit, you can't actually see anything with your eyes, but you can feel the energy of the people who are with you. What kind of energy do you want to be surrounded by? How would you feel if everybody were to gather around you and unload their pain on you? I don't think I would like that. Furthermore, it would not be a good way for those around you to send you off or say good-bye to you. The dying moment is a very special moment for the person facing it. It is the most crucial and critical moment in that person's life.

Think how wonderful it would be at the time of death if you were surrounded by happy and peaceful people who are blessing you with the positive energy of love and peace. If, instead of being surrounded by angry, frightened, or sad people, you were to be surrounded by people with love, caring, and smiles, you could leave with some lightness of heart.

Therefore, when a beloved friend or relative is dying, we must remember that even though they are unconscious, they can hear and feel us. We should utter the things that will bring comfort and peace to that person. We should not inflict our grief or fear on the person who is going through the most important transition, from this life to the next. If the dying person needs anything at all, it is our blessings and the energy of peace to make a tranquil transition. If we fail to provide that comfort at that critical moment, I think we are failing to use the last opportunity available on this earth to interact positively with that person.

In Buddhism, we believe that the last thoughts of the dying person are the most important in determining that person's next birth. If our words, thoughts, and actions at that moment contribute to creating the conditions for wholesome thoughts in the dying person's mind, wouldn't that be the best gift we can give to the departing person?

DEATH IN PERSPECTIVE

There is an undeniable, fundamental truth about life. It is the fact that nobody can guarantee we will be granted another day to live.

During sleep, our dreams seem real to us. It is only when we wake up and leave the dream behind that we are able to see that what we thought was real is not in fact so.

Only then can we understand how disjointed and cluttered the dream really was.

Life—the way we experience and interpret it—is somewhat akin to a dream. If those who have died could come back to tell us about their lives, they would say they had not been in touch with reality during their lifetime, and that their experiences were full of confusion. The message: We, the living, are not in touch with reality.

Why aren't we in touch with reality? Because we mistakenly think that this life and its attachments are permanent and that we are abiding entities. The confusion makes us cling to our property, money, and loved ones and proclaim ownership of them, which only invites fear, hatred, jealousy, and greed.

The secret of overcoming the fear of death is to understand not so much what death is, but the impermanent nature of life. Once we understand that impermanence, we can begin to accept death as a part of life, instead of seeing it as the opposite of life. That acceptance will change our attitude toward death, for we will begin to see death not as a dreaded intruder but as an expected relative. With that genuine change of attitude, we will no longer fear death.

When I was giving a lecture once, somebody said to me: "If I do not fear death, then I would easily be able to kill myself." I responded that suicide is possible not because you do not fear death, but because you fear life. Those who are in harmony with life will not fear its challenges. They will not consider suicide as a solution or even as an option, realizing the absurdity of trying to interfere with the natural flow of life.

UNDERSTANDING DEATH
THROUGH LIFE

Those who do not make any effort to understand life will have difficulty understanding death. Although we have separated life and death as opposites, they are the same thing. Birth and death are two ends of the same stick. Wherever there is life, there is death. Death is not the opposite of life; it is life itself.

Once, as a spiritual counselor, I visited with an AIDS patient in a hospice. His condition had progressed to an advanced stage; he was dying, and he knew that. We talked privately and he shared some personal thoughts with me. His voice was frail, and he spoke slowly and with difficulty. He talked about his friends and family, his concerns about their feelings, and how they were going to face his wasting body and his final moments.

I was surprised that he was not talking about his own feelings about death, so I asked him, "How do you feel about your death? Are you ready to leave this body?" He said: "When I found out that I was dying, I deeply contemplated my life and the nature of all life. And I talked with people like yourself about my thoughts. I slowly began to discover things about life that I never knew before. Now I am very excited about what is left of my life, and I don't think death can take away that excitement. You asked me whether I am ready. Yes, Bhante, I am now ready to leave this body whenever the time arrives because I am no longer afraid of either life or death. I have accepted both."

I was struck by his strength, serenity, and clarity. As I

left him I contemplated his inspiring words and thought: "Yes, he is right. Those who reject death have accepted life only partially." One cannot accept life and reject death, for they are one and the same. If one rejects death, one has to reject life also. If one accepts life, one has to accept death also.

DADDY, WHY DID MOMMY DIE?

A man came to see me with his three-year-old daughter. His wife had recently died of cancer and he was still grieving intensely. The man told me he was very concerned about his daughter and he didn't know how to explain his wife's death to her. He said he didn't know how to answer her question: "Daddy, why did Mommy die?" After thinking for a while, he had told her that she died because "everybody dies." Then he said, "I cried and she cried with me for a long time. After a few days, she asked again, 'Daddy, where did Mommy go when she died?' I told her Mommy went to heaven, and again we both cried. Every time she asks questions I feel helpless, and I hold her and cry."

I asked him whether he had given any serious thought to his daughter's questions; they were important questions, ones he should ask himself. When there are challenges like this in life, we should try to operate with a simplified mind. We should ask ourselves the questions of a child and find simple answers that would satisfy a child. Then we may find more strength and clarity to overcome our pain and unnecessary suffering.

When Bob's daughter asked him, "Why did Mommy die?" he gave a simple answer because a child cannot understand complicated ones: "Mommy died because everybody dies." If we can understand the true meaning of this simple answer, it can enlighten us greatly. If a person can understand that everybody dies, and that anybody can die at any time, including oneself, it can lighten one's attitude toward death. If everybody dies, what is the special reason that I, out of billions of people on this planet, should be spared death? The absurdity of denying death becomes obvious.

Everybody dies because death is as natural as birth. Do we ask why a baby is born? "How," maybe, but not "why." Yet it's hard for us to accept death as a natural thing. Nature's way is not something we can fight, struggle with, or change. All we can do is accept it, and only in acceptance lies peace.

Science has succeeded in prolonging life artificially even while a person may continue to suffer. I think this is a false way of dealing with life, as if it were a contest to see who can last the longest. It creates spiritual unease.

Mourning death is an emotional habit created by social conditioning. People are culturally conditioned to forget that death exists and to live as if people never die. They are also conditioned to take death with surprise, as if it never happens normally, and to weep and mourn about it. Because of this, many people become emotionally shattered. However, those who have spiritually advanced and overcome social conditioning and who are in harmony with nature's way will not be shattered by death.

We must remember that children learn how to react or

respond to any situation from their environment. Naturally, the behavior of adults is closely monitored and adopted by children. Not only adults but even children will inevitably witness death. The death of people, animals, or any living entity is not something that can ever be avoided.

The best way to teach children to accept death is to show them by example. If you believe that death should be accepted with dignity, respect, and peace, children will learn how to accept death with the same attitude. When those children become adults and meet death, they will accept it as part of life. The result will be a calm, peaceful, and dignified way of facing death, one that will be carried into future generations instead of perpetuating the morbid way of facing death that we see today.

CHOOSING TO DIE
WITH A SMILE

I have met many people who have found themselves stricken with an unexpected, life-threatening illness or accident. I quite often spend long hours talking with and counseling them. I have seen many people with strength and courage find peace in their own death. Yet sometimes I find those for whom my empathy and love can do very little to take away fear and anger. Knowing they are dying is frightening to them. Why is the discovery that they are dying the most dreadful news for most people to bear?

Once I was flying from Bangkok, Thailand, to Sri Lanka. When the plane took off, it was almost full. About half an hour into the flight, the plane suddenly dropped down a long way due to an engine problem. The plane was turning at the same time. No announcement was made to explain what had occurred. Many people panicked, screamed, and demanded an explanation of what was happening.

The American man sitting next to me was screaming and very disturbed. I lowered my eyes and relaxed my body. While still being alert to any possible instructions, I smiled to myself and felt peaceful. I didn't pay much attention to the reaction of those around me. Finally the pilot was able to get the plane under control and land safely at the airport. We all were very lucky.

When we were deplaning, the man said to me: "Are you out of your mind, or don't you care if you die? What made you smile while the plane was going down? I thought we all were going to die. Pardon me if I insult you, but you acted like a very stupid man. You didn't care to do anything about what was happening. Tell me, is that the way you monks are supposed to act in a life-threatening situation?"

I smiled again and looked at him happily. He was still restless and upset. I told him, "Well, I did not mean to laugh at the incident or deny the possible danger. However, at that moment I thought that if I were to die, I wanted to die happily and peacefully." I added, "You know, if the plane had crashed, we both might have died. I would have died happily and peacefully, and you would have died in anger and fear; I would have died with a smile, and you would have died screaming."

If I knew that I was dying and had a choice of dying

happily and peacefully or dying with fear and anger, I would definitely choose the former. That is what I did in the plane. It is my sincere hope that my life will never end trembling in fear of death, no matter how death may come to me.

PRAYING FOR HEAVEN

There was once a very faithful Christian family. When the old grandmother died, her six-year-old granddaughter was very confused about the death. The mother wanted to explain to the young daughter what had happened to her grandmother, so she said, "Sweetheart, your grandmother died and went to heaven." With spontaneous excitement, the child asked, "Mommy, why did she go to heaven?" The mother, with a great sense of relief, answered, "Well, Grandma went to heaven to be an angel."

The granddaughter smiled with all her heart. Grandma had told her many stories about heaven and angels. She had a lot of good memories of the times she spent listening to the beautiful stories. The child thought that angels were very happy people and that they were beautiful and nice.

Now she was very excited and happy about the death of her grandmother. After all, Grandma was in heaven as an angel. She was in a very nice place, much better than this world. So she asked her mother, "Mommy, shouldn't we all go to heaven and be angels?" And the mother answered, "No, dear, not until we die."

That evening, in her prayers, the child said, "Please God, help all my family to die so that they can go to heaven, too." Obviously, she was not asking God's help for everybody to die right away, but rather when each person's turn comes.

Although her prayers didn't make sense to the adults, in her innocence she accepted death as something good. She was old enough to know that her grandmother would not come back again, but it didn't matter because Grandma was an angel in heaven.

This story illustrates how much of an effect our beliefs have in forming the feelings of children, feelings they eventually carry into adulthood. If we are taught to celebrate death with good feelings when we are young, then as adults we will be able to accept death with peace and equanimity.

WHY FEAR DEATH?

I know a monk who is one hundred years old. He lives in Sri Lanka and is a very happy and peaceful person. He talks about death very comfortably. In fact, he often jokes about his own death. He said to me: "I have nothing that belongs to me in this world. Because of that, I don't have to worry about leaving it. I will gladly leave this weak and old shell whenever I have to. Until then, I will live happily and do whatever I can to help others to live peacefully." He has written many books and given them to publishers for free distribution. This very happy person has never had bank accounts or material possessions.

It is very inspiring to see old, happy, and wise people who have grown up with age and in harmony with the way life is, with nature's way. Whenever I think about my own life and old age, I hope I can live like them—that is, if I live to be that old.

I had a good friend who was in his forties. He had AIDS and was dying. I spent a lot of time with him while he was bedridden and going through a difficult struggle to live. He was always frightened to think of his death. When I made any attempt to talk about it, he refused to participate in the discussion, and he would immediately change the subject.

As far as I know, all the way into the last moment of his life he lived in fear of death and with the illusion of survival. He was clinging to his body and was trying to cling to his life. He could not think of anything beyond those two entities. When he finally had to go, it was as though he was forced out of his body against his will, rather than undergoing a voluntary and peaceful departure. Moments prior to his death, I felt helpless because I could not convince him to accept death harmoniously and die peacefully.

There are two possible attitudes toward death. One is of peace and harmony, and one is of fear and turmoil. You can face death with fear, considering it a devil, or face it with peace, considering it an angel.

How would you feel if you not only believed but knew through self-awareness that this body is a temporary home? Isn't the attachment to this body caused by the lack of awareness of our relationship with it? If we had a peaceful relationship with our body, then when nature signaled us to leave it, we would be able to do so calmly and, depending on our individual level of enlightenment, maybe even joyfully.

THE FINAL MOMENTS

Clinically, a person is considered dead when the heartbeat stops, breathing ceases, and the pupils become dilated with no response to light. Do you ever wonder what your experience of life in the last few moments will be? What will you be feeling? In this mysterious moment, you will actually become free from your identity as you know it. You have had a certain image of who you are. But that image will exist no more. You will be in your karmic energy field, and that is what you will be experiencing.

As the body begins to lose its strength and the heart stops, you will experience yourself in the mirror of your own conscience. That critical moment is given great significance in Eastern spiritual teaching. In the last moment before death, the karmic forces—that is, the consequences of all your wholesome (good) and unwholesome (evil) actions from this life, and maybe from prior lifetimes—are brought together in the awareness of your consciousness. One who is just going through the transition (death) is like a person who is leaving one country for good to settle in another country and who is allowed to take not the things he owned but only what the law permits. In this greater journey, what the law allows the person to take are only the karmic forces one has collected thus far, not material things such as house, family, or money. When you die, you will have to leave all that behind.

As a person takes the last few breaths, in the depth of his or her consciousness a lot of things begin to happen. As the body becomes still, the consciousness will gather all its energy. Whatever the dominant energies at the moment happen to be, they will be experienced in symbolic manifestations. In Buddhism, we call this *karma nimitta*. If your karmic past is dominated by positive energy, they will be experienced as pleasant and calming symbols such as beautiful colors, a light, or flowers. If the energy is negatively charged, you might see darkness and distracting symbols such as monsters, weapons, or fire. Next, you will see the place or form that this energy is going to attract for the next birth. In Buddhism, that awareness of the place where you are going to be born is called *gati nimitta*. As soon as these signs are experienced, the last thought-moment rises in you, and you will immediately be attracted to the next birth.

The last thought-moment is crucial in determining the next birth because that is what holds the power to attract the new physical form and place. As soon as the consciousness is freed from the body, it is freed also from the worldly yardsticks of time and space. The power of the last thought-moment can take one's consciousness anyplace instantly. Thus, even if the consciousness were to appear in a place many millions of miles away, it would take no time as humans know it.

Purity of mind and clarity of thought are very important at the moment of death if you are to attract a higher form of life or more comfortable conditions. Attachment to, or desire for, any worldly material things at the moment of death can pollute the stream of thoughts and may cause you to come back as a lost spirit. For example, if you die being too attached to your house, you might come back as a *peta,* which is an unfortunate being (some might call it an evil spirit) who suffers greatly because of his inability to free himself from his emotional bondage to the house. Then we say that the house is possessed.

AFTER THE FUNERAL

At the funeral, we say our final good-bye to the person who has passed on. Although the person has already left the body days earlier, this is the time when we customarily part from any physical remains. As long as the body is with us, we feel a sense of the person's existence. We experience only an incomplete separation. The lifeless body is the evidence that reminds us of the life lived in that body.

To those continuing on this life's journey, the funeral is an emotionally trying time. Their hearts are heavy, their minds confused. Long faces, sobbing, screaming, sadness, and at times silence fill the air at the graveside. After the funeral they continue to mourn, and some go on living in deep sadness for months or even years.

I was once talking to a grieving young man whose girlfriend had died in an accident. He missed her terribly, was confused, and was deeply in pain. He said he didn't want to go on like this and felt helpless. After talking to him for a while, I gave him a piece of paper. I asked him to take a few breaths, relax for a moment, and write a few things to describe why he felt so much pain.

He wrote:

We loved each other, and I terribly, terribly miss her.

I can't believe that I will never see her again. We were made for each other, but now we are separated forever.

I would like to be with her, but I can't.

I wanted to share my life with her and have a future together, but I can't.

I don't know whether I will be able to love anybody else as much as I loved her.

Then we began to discuss what he'd written. I said, "Let us carefully look at what you wrote here. It is you who are doing the worrying, not her. In this writing and in our conversation all that I hear is *I, I, I* and *me, me, me*. What I understand is that she is no longer here to fulfill your dreams, expectations, and desires, and because of that you hurt. Is this mourning a way of punishing yourself for not getting what you want? Isn't it obvious that you are crying not for her but for yourself? Your personal desires and selfish interests have caused you to be disappointed. Now you are disappointed with yourself and also with her. Isn't that the root cause of your pain?"

Then I added, "You are not deliberately being selfish, and you are not intentionally thinking that you want to cry and feel sad for yourself. But if you think deeply and realistically, you will see that the truth is that you are causing your own suffering. I am not saying that it is wrong or bad. However, if you want to overcome the suffering and go on with your life, you need to accept the natural law of death that she succumbed to, stop clinging, and regain your freedom in harmony with nature's laws.

"Sorrow, sadness, and pain are often mistakenly interpreted as signs of love for the dead person. Yet as you begin to explore those feelings intimately, you will find that grief and sorrow are ways of expressing guilt, shame, or anger toward the dead person. By saying or implying things such as 'Why did you desert me? You are not here for me. I am here without all that you could give me,' you prolong self-punishment."

I spent a long time talking to him because I felt he needed that attention to feel better. On certain important points, I took extra care to ensure that he understood clearly what I was trying to convey. For example, I was not implying that it is wrong to feel what he was feeling, or that mourning is unnecessary or bad. As ordinary human beings, we are not equipped emotionally to face such challenges with perfect balance. There are many ways to work with the sadness and deep pain of death. I had great respect for his emotions.

As we continued to meet and talk, I was happy to notice gradual progress in him. By bringing awareness to his emotions, he could feel better and happier. In any challenging situation in life, you need to get closer to the truth to liberate yourself from unnecessary pain and suffering. This may not be easy to do, but as with many other painful things in life, here too one has to work with diligence and patience to get over the suffering.

MUSTARD SEEDS

When the Buddha was alive, a young mother named Kisa Gotami lost her only child. We all can understand how terrifying it would be for any mother to see her child die. Because of her intense love and affection for the child, she lost her mind. In that state, she believed that the child was just ill, and she was determined to find a cure. She carried the body on her shoulder and roamed the city, asking each person she met to heal her child. A wise man who understood her distorted emotions sent her to the Buddha.

Holding the corpse in her arms, she arrived at a beautiful park where the Buddha was teaching. The moment she saw the Buddha, she appealed to Him to heal the child. The Buddha compassionately understood her emotional state. Without mentioning anything about a cure, the Buddha said, "Your child has died, but before I do anything about it, please go and collect some mustard seeds from a house where no one has ever died."

Happily she thanked the Buddha and took off on her mission. Her mind now filled with hope, she went from house to house asking for mustard seeds. Every house she went to had mustard seeds, but she could not find a single house where there had been no death. Eventually the truth dawned on her. The grief and the pain of losing her beloved child faded away. She understood her own insanity.

That deep awareness of death brought her not only emotional healing of her personal trauma but also an understanding of the true nature of life. The awareness of death gave her a sense of peace and harmony. She properly disposed of the corpse of her child and came back to the Buddha.

The Buddha knew of her transformation. He counseled her and delivered a *dharma* discourse on the nature of things. Inspired by the wisdom of the teachings, she asked the Buddha to ordain her as a nun. After becoming a nun, she meditated on death and, realizing the impermanent nature of all existence, she attained enlightenment.

For twenty-five hundred years, Kisa Gotami has been one of the most famous enlightened nuns in Buddhist history. All the Buddhist children in Sri Lanka learn her life story. When I learned it, I was about eight years old. It is a story that I have heard many times. Each time I hear it and contemplate its message of impermanence, death, and the implications that follow, it adds another layer of profoundness to the meaning of life. For this woman, the move from ignorance to complete awareness of the truth of her child's death brought liberation and enlightenment.

We too must train ourselves to awaken to the profound lessons about the realities of life that are hidden within the experience of death. These lessons are waiting to lift us from the grief that is sapping our energy; they are there to nurture us and to make our continuing journey, and that of those around us, joyous and meaningful. To realize this, we need to go beyond the pain of our emotions and let a spark of truth touch our hearts, as it did Kisa Gotami's. After all, wouldn't that also be a beautiful gift to give to our departed ones?

REFLECTION ON DEATH

This is a simple exercise that I sometimes lead people through to encourage them to examine their feelings and beliefs about death. Hard though it may seem initially, this is something we all need to do as often as possible. What we are trying to do is slowly, with practice, change our mind-set from a pretense (that death does not exist or that it is an insignificant event far, far away somewhere) to a reality.

Try to remind yourself about the truth of your own death in a peaceful but honest way, and train your mind to be aware of it in a comfortable manner. Properly practiced, awareness of death brings immense strength and wisdom to life by removing the erroneous past conditioning that we should treat death as an enemy and with fear.

At first you may feel somewhat uncomfortable with this exercise, depending on your disposition. However, with time you will begin to feel increasingly comfortable with it. Eventually you not only will be at ease with the exercise, but also will benefit from the tranquility added to your life as a result of coming to realistic terms with death.

Relax the body, sit comfortably, and connect with yourself intimately. Close your eyes. Imagine that you are only seven days away from your death. Just one week to live. What are your feelings about the end of your life? Are you afraid even to think about death? You have to leave everything and everybody behind. How would you feel about leaving everybody and everything forever, at least in the context of your present existence and relationships? Do you feel sad or angry or afraid?

At this stage, I want you to stay with your feelings without making any effort to change them. You don't have to judge them as good or bad. You must accept honestly how you are feeling about leaving everybody and everything as you die. Direct your mind away from any distractions and stay with your feelings until you clearly experience them.

Remove your attention slowly from those feelings and imagine that you are only four days away from your death. How do you feel about the way you have lived your life? This time, try to reflect on your relationship with your family and friends. Are you satisfied with the way you have treated them? Or the way they have treated you? Do you feel there is unfinished business? And is there time to attend to it?

What are the areas that you would have improved to bring more satisfaction and peace? Remain with your feelings without trying to change them.

Now, imagine that you are only two days away from the final good-bye. You have only forty-eight hours to live. Reflect on how you would want everybody—your friends and family—to treat you. How close do you want them to be to you? What kind of feelings would you like them to have? Do you want to see them sad, happy, or neutral emotionally? What kind of advice would you give them to help them accept your death and make them feel better? This is only an exploration of your feelings, so you do not need to correct anything that you feel. Stay with your feelings for a few minutes.

Finally, go to the last day of your life. You now have just twenty-four hours left. How are you feeling about your death? Is there frustration, rage, or disappointment? Are you afraid to face the final moments? Are you afraid of what might happen after death? Do you feel any peace or harmony at all? Closely observe your feelings for as long as you wish. Do not make any effort to change them. All that you need to do in this exercise is to bring your feelings to your attention.

When you are done, keep your eyes closed and let your mind wander for another minute or two. Do not focus on any specific questions at this stage. When you feel like it, open your eyes.

If you like, you can keep a journal of your emotional responses each time you try this reflection. If done with proper absorption and contemplation, you will find your emotional response changing from agitation on the first occasion to calmness and tranquility with practice.

DEATH IN EVERY MOMENT

Our tangible experience of death manifests itself as a one-time life event happening to the people we know, such as parents, other family members, and friends. However, there is another experience of death that is not obvious, visible, or felt, but is nonetheless taking place within us endlessly. I'm talking about our cells, invisible to the naked eye but, in fact, the building blocks of the visible body. These cells die every few hours, days, or years, depending on their type, and are replaced by new cells. So, although at the visible, experiential level we appear to remain the same, something of us is dying all the time and is being replaced by new life. In effect, we can say that we are actually dying innumerable times at the invisible level, although at the visible level we die only once.

We have just seen that the physical inner being is nothing but an unbroken process of birth (rising) and death (falling), and hence the manifestation of physical energy is an unbroken flow. Because the spiritual inner being is based on the physical, we can say that the former is a stream of consciousness that is constantly rising and falling, an unbroken flow of spiritual energy that resonates and is in harmony with the physical energy. Thus, just as we experience physical birth, decay, and death every moment, we experience psychological birth, decay, and death every moment. Birth and death, together with the link in between, is what we call existence. Although we cannot see it at the cellular level, birth and death are what make us who we are. For our existence to continue, birth and death must happen constantly. So, death is not the enemy we label it to be, but an essential determinant of our existence. Put another way, existence has two parents—birth and death, and both of them are responsible for what we are. We cannot love one parent and hate the other. To be in touch with reality, we need to welcome death, just as we welcome birth.

It is simply a lack of awareness of this most natural of phenomena—of birth, change, decay, and death—that blinds us to its presence amidst all of us. This is why the All, the Enlightened One, the Buddha, advised monks to accept the fact of life and death with equanimity and mindfulness. That acceptance is a spiritual awakening that leads us to serenity.

THE HEAVENS AND HELLS

According to certain religious beliefs, heaven and hell are two different places where the dead will find their eternal home. After death, on the day of judgment, you will be sent to either heaven or hell for eternity. Although the words *heaven* and *hell* are familiar to Buddhists, we use them in a different context. Buddhists believe in heavens and hells.

For a Buddhist, a heaven and a hell could be either actual physical places, with physical forms, or a nonphysical existence. Think of a place where living beings do not experience any emotional suffering or physical pain. Their physical body is so subtle that it cannot feel pain as ours does. Their emotional existence is so advanced that they do not experience emotional suffering, either. Their minds are so advanced psychically that they are fully aware of the true nature of their existence. Therefore, they live in harmony with nature. Buddhists believe that there are many such places in this complex, vast universe. We call them *deva* worlds or *brahma* worlds.

We use the word *heavens* to imply such places where happiness, peace, and harmony would be the experience of those who live in them. Those who are born in these places do not live forever, just as we don't. Therefore, just like earthlings, they will face death when their karma dictates and will be born again. Some of us might have experienced heavens in our previous births.

The experience of time for beings born into *deva* or *brahma* worlds will be different from our experience of time because time is only an experience relative to where we are in this universe. In terms of our time, these other beings might live hundreds or even thousands of years. To those beings, in experiential measure, thousands of years may not mean a long time.

The hells (*apayas*, in Pali) also are many. Think, for example, of what happened with the famine in Ethiopia. For many years, children were born in suffering, lived in suffering, and died in suffering. This suffering was due to the lack of the very basic needs for survival. When living beings are born into pain, and live and die in pain, we say that they live in hell. If an entire planet is engulfed in a famine, we can say that the world (the planet) itself is hell and a person born into these circumstances is born in hell. Given the likelihood that other beings exist elsewhere in the universe, there are likely to be as many such hells as there are heavens. Buddhists would say that those charged with negative karmic energy are attracted to such places and could experience immense pain until they die.

The living beings who are born in *apayas* (hells) are also not there forever. As soon as their negative karma is spent, they will die and continue the journey of life. We all might have experienced heavens and hells in our previous births. And we may experience them again in our future lives. The heavens and hells are not the only two places that one can be born in after death. There could be many other places in between those two extreme conditions. Also, life could exist even without a physical world. We call such existence the formless realm.

When we think of planet Earth and human beings, we realize that every human is capable of creating the experience of hell or heaven. Heavenly comforts and hellish pain could be experienced either momentarily and temporarily, or over one's entire life span. External comforts alone do not help to create heaven or hell. It is more of a psychological state of mind. To repeat Milton's words, "The mind . . . in itself can make a heav'n of hell, a hell of heav'n." Living in a mansion with all the money in the world will not guarantee the experience of heaven. People who live in extreme luxury may never have a heavenly experience if they do not experience inner spiritual comfort and peace.

Referring to harmonious, loving, and peaceful relationships between men and women, the Buddha on many occasions mentioned an "angel living with an angel." In this sense, heaven and hell are experiences that each human being is capable of creating for himself or herself on planet Earth in this lifetime. Every human being is equipped with the inner powers to create either experience.

SHARING THE MERITS

Buddhists believe that they can give a great gift to the departed ones. This gift is to perform "acts of merit" and transfer those merits to the departed ones. The purpose of the Buddhist funeral ceremony is to share the merits and to wish them a happy and trouble-free onward journey.

At a funeral in Sri Lanka, monks lead the participants through several simple rituals to symbolically transfer merits to the dead person before the body is cremated or buried. Every Buddhist considers these rituals very important and that it is their duty to perform them. While the departed person might benefit from the shared energy, such ceremonies bring enormous release to those who are alive, helping heal their pain and grief.

At the moment of the ceremony, Buddhists are discouraged from weeping, feeling sorry, lamenting, or bewailing. This is because such behavior brings no good consequences for the departed. One's state of mind has to be undistracted and positive for the best results. It is like charging your mind with positive, wholesome thoughts and sharing those thought waves with the departed person. It may be a little like sharing blessings with a sick person. When somebody is ill, we go to them and bless them with the healing energy of our positive thoughts. We send our blessings or pray for them so they can get well.

The funeral service begins with reciting the Five Precepts. They are not to kill, not to steal, not to lie, to shun sexual misconduct, and not to use any intoxicating drinks or drugs. It is a way of establishing ourselves in virtue. Then comes the offering of robes to the monks. Afterward, the monks will chant and the attending people will listen to some verses from the teachings of the Buddha that remind them of the impermanent nature of all existence. While the monks are chanting, the participants will be silent and reflect meditatively on the chanting. The reflection and meditation are supposed to bring calmness and peace to the minds of the participants.

The highlight of the funeral ceremony is the actual moment of transferring the merits. We place an empty cup and a jug of water by the coffin. All the friends and relatives of the departed person will hold the jug of water. They recall all the meritorious and wholesome deeds that he or she performed and pour water into the empty cup, reciting a verse that says: "May the departed person receive the energies of our wholesome and pure thoughts and be well and happy on the journey of life." They pour water into the empty cup until it overflows.

The funeral ceremony is followed by an alms-giving ceremony on the seventh day after the death, then another three months later, and annually thereafter. The family members of the departed invite the monks to the alms-giving ceremony, feed them, and listen to chanting of the scriptures and a sermon. Then at the end they perform the ritual to transfer the merits. Feeding the relatives and guests toward the end of the ceremony is also a big part of the event.

In Buddhist practice, one important way the living friends and relatives remember the departed is to perform good and meritorious deeds in their memory. On each remembrance day, the family members and relatives invite the monks, feed them, and offer them their basic necessities. Other meritorious activities may include a visit to a hospital to offer medicine to sick people, releasing captive birds into freedom, feeding the poor, and providing essentials to the needy.

CHAPTER SEVEN

The Law of Karma

That which ye sow ye reap. See yonder fields!
The sesamum was sesamum, the corn
was corn. The silence and the Darkness knew!
So is a man's fate born.

SIR EDWIN ARNOLD, *Light of Asia*

⚞ A S K   Y O U R S E L F ⚟

*I*n Buddhist and Hindu countries in Southeast Asia, karma *is a common word used in day-to-day language. People have been using the word for thousands of years. Only in the recent past was it introduced to the West. Since then, more and more people in the West are beginning to use this word, often with different interpretations.*

If you have ever heard of karma, does it mean anything to you? If you happen to believe in karma, please take a few minutes to explore your understanding of it. Obviously, you are familiar with terms such as fate, will of God, *and* destiny. *Does karma relate to the meanings of any of these?*

When you reflect on your life, are you aware of how and why certain things happen as they do? Can you describe that awareness? Do you think that everything in life is accidental, or do you think that things happen according to the plan of a higher power?

Do you believe in rebirth? If so, do you think that the consequences of your past karma (actions) can be experienced in this life, and the consequences of actions in this life will be experienced in future lives? In other words, do you think the forces of karma could travel from life to life?

THE LAW OF
CAUSE AND EFFECT

Before we explore this fascinating subject, let me tell you a story from my childhood, when I was first exposed to the idea of karma.

When I was a little boy, I often heard my mother make remarks like, "Son, you have done good karma today" or "Son, don't do that, it is bad karma." I didn't question her as to what karma was because, even as a little boy, I knew that karma related to the good and bad things I did. That was a sufficient definition for me at that time.

Through a personal conviction as a devout Buddhist, my mother refrained from boiling eggs, even though there were other Buddhists who did not believe anything was spiritually wrong with boiling eggs. In our village we had country eggs, which were fertile and therefore contained unborn life capable of hatching as chicks. So my mother believed that boiling an egg killed an unborn life.

One day I asked her why she wouldn't boil eggs. She said, "Son, it is bad karma to boil eggs." Then I asked her what she meant by bad karma. Explaining, she said: "It is bad karma to hurt others. If you hurt others, it comes back to you, and then you will be hurt, too." Driven by that simple but wonderful and convincing explanation, I have always tried my utmost not to hurt any living beings.

Many years later, as a novice teenage monk at the temple, I studied karma in detail. When I was a very young boy, I believed in good and bad and their relationship to karma simply because adults whom I respected, including my parents, believed that way. Now, having studied the Buddhist doctrine, I still believe in the same practical essence of karma, but my understanding is much deeper and more meaningful. Today, this understanding of karma has helped me make sense of many things I would otherwise have difficulty understanding or explaining. It has provided me with much motivation to find ways to live my life with love, compassion, and peace.

Karma simply means "action." It is a Sanskrit word that can mean any physical, mental, or verbal act. But modern Buddhists use this word in a special sense to mean both actions and reactions, or cause and effect of our mental energy. The Buddha used two terms: *karma*, meaning "action," and *vipaka*, meaning "consequence."

In the language of science, karma is called the law of cause and effect. Buddhists quite often use the term *moral causation.* Moral causation is said to work in the moral realm just as the physical law of action and reaction works in the physical realm. An unbroken sequence of causes and effects occurs in the mental and moral sphere just as strictly as in the physical realm.

The Buddha defined karma as "motive" (*chetana*). In the doctrine of karma, the Buddha discusses motivated verbal, physical, and mental actions and their consequences. Action is of three kinds—wholesome karma, unwholesome karma, and neutral action. The doctrine of karma is, in short, that our thoughts are responsible for our destiny in life.

The doctrine of karma puts an enormous responsibility on the individual for the shaping of his or her own destiny in the remainder of this life and future lives. Accordingly, it places great emphasis on the need for an individual to practice self-restraint and to use his or her will and energies for wholesome living that is conducive to spiritual progress.

Obviously, the law of karma existed before the Buddha—in fact, from the beginning of the universe. The Buddha *discovered* the universal law of karma, particularly as it applies to the human mind, including the operating principle of associated karmic energy. He made us aware of how this energy contributes to the making and shaping of our experience of life. In basic and simple terms, the Buddha stated the law thus: "As you sow the seeds, so shall you reap the fruit." If you sow bad seeds, you will reap a bad harvest, and if you sow good seeds, you will reap a good harvest.

All emotionally motivated mental, physical, or verbal actions comprise active karma. Actions that are produced without the involvement of emotional motivation are not considered active karma. If no energy has been produced out of your emotions, there is nothing to come back to you. Such actions are called *neutral actions*.

When I was teaching at a spiritual study center in New York, one staff member who was also a student of mine came to me upset and crying. She said that she had done something terrible and she considered it to be bad karma. She said, "When I was driving on a country road, I ran over a raccoon and killed it. By that killing I have created bad karma for myself."

Obviously, she didn't have a proper understanding of karma. She felt responsible for the death and had been saddened by it, and she thought that death resulting from any action was bad karma.

I asked her: "Did you have any intention of killing the raccoon?" She said she didn't. I asked her whether she had been driving carelessly, and her answer was again no. It was obvious that the killing of the animal was a neutral action and that she was not aware of the existence of the three different types of actions. Since her emotional energy had not been involved in the act of killing, she was free of both responsibility for the death and the consequences. I explained the three types of karma to her and consoled her by saying, "Don't worry about the karma. Just try to get over your sadness, because you are not responsible for the raccoon's death."

We explored her feelings further, and she was able to overcome some of her sadness and guilt. I further eased her mind by suggesting that the karma of the raccoon was such that it had to die at that time, and if she had not run over it, it could have died some other way.

Of the three types of actions, neutral action does not involve emotional energy and therefore brings no consequences. The other two, wholesome and unwholesome karma, are produced from the emotional energy of motivation and are therefore followed by consequences.

Any action that is driven by a pure, peaceful, and positive state of mind is a wholesome action. The nature of energy carried by wholesome karma is such that it causes no harm to anyone. Instead, what follows from wholesome karma is pure joy.

Wholesome actions also result in spiritual comfort. Because such actions are motivated by love and care, with no expectation of returns, there is no stress in the action. Thus, the results have to be comforting.

Actions driven by impure thoughts or distracted, negative states of mind result in unwholesome karma. They have the power to cause hurt or pain to oneself and others. For example, take something you have decided to do for a parent. If you set about doing it reluctantly, or out of obligation, or just to avoid blame, then although you may physically accomplish the task, it leaves you with a sense of mental discomfort or even unhappiness. These are the discernible manifestations of the unwholesome karma associated with the deed.

On the other hand, if you carry out this deed for your parent with love, care, and appreciation, you will physically accomplish the same result. Yet in addition, and more important, you will feel mentally joyous, happy, and noble

about what you have done. These are the discernible manifestations of the wholesome karma underlying the deed this
time. A deed done with impure intentions adds unwholesome karma to your existing karmic collection, whereas one
carried out with pure and noble intentions adds wholesome
karma.

The doctrine of karma teaches us about the importance
of every thought and action in our day-to-day living.
Therefore, we should endeavor to be constantly mindful of
our thoughts and the actions that follow these thoughts.

MAKING CHOICES

Making the right choice is a challenge in every moment of
our lives. Conscious and unconscious choices we make
motivate our actions. Thoughts, emotions (feelings), and
physical actions are results of the choices we make. Some of
these choices are made deliberately, with conscious awareness. Others are made very rapidly, without much awareness. Oftentimes we are not aware of how we make those
choices. The act of making a conscious choice is called
chetana in Buddhism. Without *chetana* there is no karma.

According to the Buddhist Doctrine of Dependent
Arising, whenever A occurs, B occurs, and whenever A does
not occur, B does not occur; thus, A and B are causally
related. Such a theory of causality is compatible with free
will. In this context, free will means the ability to navigate
the direction of your life using the control you have over
your present-moment karma.

As you make conscious choices, your mental energy gets actively engaged in your thoughts and actions. The choices you make prepare the mind to act. Mental actions (thoughts) produce bodily or verbal actions. By making choices in your thinking, you can willfully direct your actions. If you choose to be healthy, your body and mind will act accordingly and you will have good health. When you choose love or peace, you set your mind to bring that experience to your life. In this sense, you can use the law of karma to be well or ill, happy or unhappy, rich or poor, or a good or bad person. Ultimately, your happiness and unhappiness in life are conditioned by the choices that *you* make.

Say, for example, that somebody cuts you off on the highway or speaks an insulting word at your workplace. If you choose to react angrily, then you will create the experience of discomfort, pain, or unhappiness for yourself. Negative reactions do not bring you any inner comfort. If you choose to respond with patience and kindness, you will experience peace, and peace offers you inner comfort. The person who speaks the insulting word to you or the one who cuts you off on the highway has provided stimulation for you to make a choice—that is, to respond positively or negatively. Whatever choice you make, you are the master of the process. Therefore, the results of your actions are yours.

If you have been abused by somebody, forgiveness can free you from the karmic bond. If you fail to make the wholesome choice of forgiving the victimizer, then you will continue to suffer from the destructive emotional energy you have created, in spite of the fact that what started the process was the act of the victimizer. If you choose to let go of feelings of revenge and anger, and forgiveness fills their place, you will free yourself from the negative cycle of karmic energy.

Forgiveness makes it possible to release the negative feelings that could result from the painful experience of past memory. Among victims, I have seen that those who choose to forgive begin to live in peace, and those who hold on to the anger or hatred and are incapable of making that choice of forgiving continue to suffer. When the victimizer walks away, the action that hurts you becomes part of the dead past, and it is up to you to make a choice to use all your strengths to forgive and let go of the hurt. Such wholesome karmic choices bless you with peace and happiness.

Try to be more aware of, and pay close attention to, the choices that you make, knowing that they shape your karmic path. The law of karma dictates that you can never run away from the consequences of your actions. That is why the Buddha said, "Not in the sky, nor in mid-ocean, nor in a mountain cave, is found that place on earth where abiding one may escape from the consequences of one's own karma."

MAKING WHOLESOME CHOICES

From time to time, we need to ask ourselves how we can consciously learn to make more wholesome choices that will enhance the quality of life. For that purpose, let's do the following exercise.

Take a pen and paper, sit down, and relax for a while.

Then reflect on the choices you made today and write them down. Which ones were made willfully—for example, going for a thirty-minute walk this morning or consciously telling an untruth? Which ones were made without much awareness—for example, putting the kettle to boil upon waking or reacting aggressively and impatiently to a spouse's mistake? Mark them as such.

Now, to the best of your ability, mark the choices that were wholesome (for example, the decision to go for a brisk walk) and the ones that were unwholesome (for example, reacting negatively to a mistake of your spouse). Add up the wholesome choices and then the unwholesome choices to get a feel for your current trend in choice making.

Next, pay attention to each of the unwholesome choices and write down the conscious wholesome choices that you can make the next time around—for example, responding calmly and positively to a mistake made by your spouse rather than reacting negatively and aggressively. Then, tomorrow and thereafter, try to put into practice the wholesome choice you have selected, in place of the old, habitual unwholesome action. After a week, reflect on your wholesome and unwholesome choices to see if you have made substantial progress in improving your choices. Repeat for a few more weeks until you find yourself making more wholesome choices than unwholesome ones, and more conscious responses than mechanical reactions.

Use the following list of tips to cultivate your awareness of the choices you make. Also, let them remind you of the limitless choice-making powers available to you for making your life fulfilling.

- When you wake up first thing in the morning, *make a conscious choice* to enjoy the blessings of the day.

- When things do not come your way as expected or people are not what you want them to be, *choose* acceptance.

- When somebody displays anger or jealousy toward you or disapproves of you, instead of reacting with anger, *consciously choose* to respond with self-confidence and calmness.

- When you get in the car, remind yourself that your *choice* is to not let those who have chosen aggression on the road take away your calmness as you drive.

- *Choose* to be mindful of your daily conduct so that you will never hurt anybody with your thoughts, speech, and actions.

PAST KARMA

I know many who mistakenly believe that karma means *only* the consequences of the things, often bad things, that they have done in their past lives. Led by such beliefs, when something goes wrong they say, "I might have done something terrible in one of my past lives to deserve this experience." Yes, there are forces of our past lives that may bring us painful or pleasurable experiences in this life. Nevertheless, our past-life karma is not the sole director of our experiences in this life.

Past karma is only one factor that influences our present (and future) life. Our present action (present karma) is the other, more critical factor from the point of view of life's direction. It is present action, not past action, that one has control of to change the course of one's destiny. So, the only true savior is one's present karma, which is under the control of one's will, and not an external, all-powerful deity or other entity. It is also because of the power and potential of present karma that one does not have to be a slave to one's past karma or live only to pay for past actions.

According to Buddhist teaching, past karma means all your mental and physical acts prior to this moment and their associated consequences or results. In this sense, if you stole a hundred dollars from your company a week ago and now your boss fires you for that action, then your being fired now is the present consequence of the past karma of stealing. That is an example of bad karma. If you studied diligently for four years and received your degree certificate, then the reward of the degree is the result of the good karma of diligent study.

When the present turns into the past, your consciousness does not lose connection with it. The threads of those unseen forces continue to influence the present and future. Although the effects of past karmic forces by themselves may generate a mix of pleasant and unpleasant experiences for you, you can steer away from the unpleasant by using your will and present karma. This can be likened to a skilled navigator who steers his ship away from the rocks in spite of a nasty storm that tries at times to force the ship toward them.

Suppose, for example, that I have done something really bad in the past. That action will send out a lot of destructive karmic energy that will make its way back to me. How this energy affects me will be based on my present state of mind. If my mind is distracted and filled with negative energy at present, it is ripe to receive that negative energy from the past. In such situations, I will experience the full effects of the forces of the past karma.

Now assume that I have a positive state of mind when the same negative energy reaches me. I am mentally focused and peaceful, and my heart is pure and clear. How the energy from the past affects me would depend on the degree of positive strength in my mind presently. If my positive energy is substantial, then the energy of the past karma could have only a minor effect on me now, or it may even dissipate completely without causing any harm to me.

The belief that one has the power to abate or nullify the negative effects of one's past unwholesome karma motivates each of us to do good when faced with challenges in life.

In Sri Lanka, when faced with an imminent crisis or a life-threatening situation, some believers first consult a reader of horoscopes to determine what kind of good deeds they should do to generate counteractive positive energy. Then, with urgency and eagerness, they follow up with action. Good deeds can include releasing caged birds or animals, or cows from the slaughterhouses; going to the temple to meditate; feeding the poor, helping the sick, or other charitable work.

These traditional practices have symbolic as well as factual significance to a Buddhist. Most people do these things out of faith rather than through reasoning. Behind the practice, there is acceptance of the past and the power that past karma might have over one. Nevertheless, we should remember that the strength of our present state of mind will always be the master of our destiny. When one understands this, there is no reason to worry unnecessarily about the past and feel as if one is a helpless victim of previous karma.

You should be prepared for anything from the mysterious past. Work on bringing wholeness to the present and purity to your heart and mind. If you are bothered by bad things done in the past, shed that worry now. It is never too late for you to turn things around by trying to do good from now on. You hold the keys to your happiness through your present actions. Do not let your past deeds or who you have been disqualify you from opening the door. You can choose to be miserable or you can choose to be happy, to be comfortable, and to enjoy peace here and now.

In my opinion, a proper understanding of the law of karma can be the greatest motivating force for a human being. The present moment holds limitless powers to control one's destiny. The winds blowing from one's past can be used to one's advantage to navigate one's life in a chosen direction. Do not surrender to past karma and feel yourself a victim. Be awake to the present and know the powers you hold herein. Then you can find peace and happiness in this very life, regardless of the nature of your karmic past.

KARMA AND ABUSE

The Buddhist doctrine of karma throws light on some interesting issues relating to abuse and other wrongdoing in relationships.

A relationship involves two parties and, therefore, the bonding of two karmas. Since the present karma of each individual goes back in an endless chain through this life and into past lives, it is beyond our comprehension to know the exact nature of the forces that are involved in bringing about the experience between two people or to know the first causes. Thus, blame—in the sense in which we commonly use the word—does not have meaning in the Buddhist doctrine of karma. In the case of abuse, all we can say is that both the victim and the victimizer were placed in the encounter by the unique nature of the combined karma, the origin of which is unfathomable.

While societal rules may bring punishment to a wrongdoer here and now, the karmic law says that an abuser will suffer the consequences in this life now or later, or in a future birth for sure, "as the wagon follows the hoof of the horse that draws it."

To put things in perspective, we should also look at the other side of the coin. If two persons' lives come together and, as a result of *positive* interactions, they are happy, we would not say that one person's happiness is the sole responsibility of the other person. It would be more appropriate to say that here too it is a unique but unfathomable karmic bonding that is "responsible" for the happiness.

For these reasons, the Buddha never advocated the

punishment of a victimizer. He taught instead how to reha-
bilitate and educate the victimizer as well as the victim.
Otherwise, the victim who is not rehabilitated and educated
can in turn become a victimizer, thus perpetrating an endless
chain of negativity.

UNRESOLVED PAST

I believe that karmically you can pick up right where you
left off in relationships from past lives. When two people are
reunited by karmic forces, they can begin the journey again
as friends or enemies. The break (repulsion) that you establish with an enemy can be as strong as the bond (attachment)
that you create with a friend. If you part from somebody
with hate, you will meet that person again with hate because
of the unresolved emotional relationship. If you part from
somebody with peace, love, and caring, when you meet that
person again you will create conditions to share the same
virtues again.

Past-life therapy is based on the notion that for some of
the difficulties and problems—physical, mental, and emotional—in our present lives, there could be a link to a past
life. The cause of the present condition may be traced back
to the past through therapy. Then, by releasing the mental
and emotional blocks, the present condition can be healed
and cured.

Once I had a wonderful opportunity to witness a
past-life therapy class. It was a five-day workshop. There
were about fifteen participants. Many came to the class in

search of solutions for problems they could not resolve through other means. I listened to a number of people who had been carrying anger and hate from their past lives into the present.

Among the many stories I heard in the therapy sessions, there was one in particular that had a strong impact on me. It was about a man who had carried into his present life the anger he had toward his son in a past life. Richard was in his forties and could not find a logical reason for his revulsion and anger toward his offspring.

He said, "My son is a fine boy and I don't understand why I hate him so much." After many years of frustration and anger, he had sought help from a number of professionals, to no avail. Finally he had come to this past-life therapy session. The class formed a circle around him and watched as he slowly drifted into his feelings of anger, making a connection to a lifetime hundreds of years back. Here is the story he related to us.

Richard is an old man who lives in a small town with his wife and only son. Unexpectedly, a war erupts and many people are killed. To save their own lives, Richard and his family decide to join many others who are escaping from the war-torn area. They pack their valuables and start the journey toward an unknown destination. Soon they find themselves in the middle of a forest surrounded by hills and mountains. As Richard, his wife, and son are fleeing through the forest, Richard falls and breaks his leg.

With the help of his wife and son, he continues his journey for a few more days until his condition worsens and prevents him from walking any farther. They hear gunfire close by. The wife and son have to make a decision either to leave Richard and flee toward freedom or stay with him and face the consequences. Richard's wife wants to stay behind, and Richard agrees. However, his son wants to leave the father behind and continue the journey with his mother. An argument ensues.

While the old man is weeping and screaming, the strong young son disappears into the forest, dragging his mother with him. Lame, sick, and sapped of energy, Richard lies on the ground with immense anger and hatred toward his son. Until he eventually dies, Richard cries in pain, cursing his son.

This tragedy happened to Richard many lifetimes ago; his son escaped from him then, but not forever. Neither could escape from his karma. They both attracted each other again in this life. Because of the interference of deep, unconscious memory, Richard could never love his son in this life. Yet his limited conscious mind could not grasp what was going on deep in his unconscious, a territory beyond his control.

Richard's conflict was between the conditioned values of his present consciousness and the memories buried deep in his unconscious. He was torn between two powerful forces. One was the conscious awareness of a father's responsibility to love and care for his son. The other was his inability to do so due to the undercurrent of karmic forces in the depths of his unconscious. Up to now he had been confused.

Richard had to relive his deep, unconscious memories and forgive his son if he was to recapture his love for him.

Only then could Richard mend the unwholesome karmic break and establish a normal loving relationship with his son.

If you harbor ill will toward your children, parents, or friends, you will cause suffering to yourself and them in this life, as well as in future lives. Whatever the reasons that attracted them into your present life, by choosing to have a wholesome, harmonious relationship with them here and now, you will not create negative karmic debts that will have to be repaid in future lives.

KARMA IS NOT FATE

To believe that past karma alone determines the course of one's life is to believe in fatalism. The Buddha's doctrine of karma is not fatalism or predestination but determinism, where everything depends on conditions. Fate is something that you cannot change. It is predetermined. You cannot change the effects of your past karma. Yet you can change the way they affect you and the direction your life takes by controlling your present karma.

There is a very popular story in Buddhist literature about a person who went through a phenomenal transformation from an evildoer to a saint. In the early part of his life he was a model of goodness and bore the name Ahinsaka, meaning "the innocent one." In school he demonstrated exceptional skill and superior intelligence in all his activities and became the favorite student of the teacher. His classmates became jealous of him and were bent on destroying the relationship between the teacher and Ahinsaka. Although their initial attempts failed, eventually they were able to mislead the teacher about Ahinsaka by inventing a false story.

After a series of episodes, the story relates how eventually Ahinsaka became a ruthless killer. He killed hundreds of people and collected the right thumb of each victim, which he wore strung on a necklace. So he came to be known as Angulimala, which means "one who wears a necklace of fingers."

On meeting the Buddha, Angulimala renounced killing. In his infinite compassion, the Fully Enlightened Buddha allowed Angulimala to become his disciple and enter the order of monks, notwithstanding the fact that he had killed hundreds of people and was wanted for murder. Angulimala became a genuine truth seeker and committed himself to follow the Buddha's path to peace. He spent many days diligently applying himself to meditation. Soon the vision of truth dawned on him, and the former killer attained awakening and became a spiritually perfect saint.

There are many such stories in Buddhist literature. Those stories tell us how people with the worst imaginable forms of behavioral problems have changed for the better and eventually attained perfection. Therefore, let's not be preoccupied with our own past mistakes, committed through ignorance. Buddhism shows how, instead of leaving one's destiny in the hands of fate, one can change as Angulimala did, through the hard work of inner transformation. Instead of being victims of past deeds, let us use the past for growth in the present.

Only you can change the effects of your past karma, and the intervention of any external force or person will be of no avail. Karmic energy, which is the energy of one's own thoughts and behavior, affects exclusively the one who thinks and behaves. There could be occasions when you have no power to change certain karmic effects. On such occasions, you may not be able to do anything about them but experience the consequences until they are over.

What is important from an individual's point of view is not the circumstance, but one's attitude to the circumstance. By changing how we view the circumstance, we can face it, no matter how bad, with an attitude that brings peace of mind. This is how present karma can transform the effects of past karma. The doer of karma has significant potential to change the direction of his or her life with the creation of wholesome present karma. We are not at the mercy of a thing called fate; instead, we are masters of our own destiny who can effectively use present action to steer our course.

KARMIC TIES

There are billions of people on this planet. Yet only a handful become the most intimate in your life. It always seems to be a mystery how and why we attract these few to share our lives. Why have you attracted to your life those human beings who now happen to be your parents, children, other relatives, and friends? Are they just accidents? What kind of deeper meanings must there be to those relationships?

In spite of the complexities and still-unresolved mysteries of life, there is a causal relationship between events in life. In very close, interactive relationships, there is a larger picture we do not see. The larger picture contains subtle forces, and one of those forces, the most important one, is karma.

When we try to understand the nature of human relationships from a karmic standpoint, we must try to go to the depths of the human psyche. Then we need to explore the powers and energies that it contains, because most of the events and awareness in one's life are brought into existence out of the depths of the psyche. Eastern philosophies have made serious efforts to explain how the inner forces of the human being interact constantly with the outer forces to make things happen.

Although not everything can be explained rationally, the psychological law of karma has made significant contributions in bringing clarity to the understanding of life. It has given us insight into the human experience and has helped us recognize the forces that are involved with it. The Buddhist theory of psychic determinism, called the Doctrine of Dependent Arising (or *paticcasamuppada*, in Pali) teaches us how the psychic forces and associated energy make life experience happen through the process of causal relationships.

In general, for life to exist, many forces must interact. The forces that are generated in the depths of the psyche are considered to be the most powerful ones that create our unique personal experience of life.

We know that enormous amounts of energy can be

generated by splitting the atom, as is done in atomic bombs and in nuclear power–generating stations. The Swiss psychologist Carl Jung suggested that comparable amounts of mental energy could be generated if the depths of the human psyche were used to full potential. Still, while relatively dormant, energies residing in the depths of the mind interact in many complex ways to create the events of our day, from minor to major.

For example, let us take a current relationship between two people and try to see how that relationship came to be, through a long chain of causal links.

Suppose that a woman goes to a party and meets an interesting man. The two start to have a conversation and suddenly begin to like each other. They make a date to meet again the following day at dinner. A few more meetings, and the two people discover that they have fallen in love.

The unique event of these two specific persons falling in love at a specific moment under specific circumstances is attributed to the effect of a multitude of karmic linkages. In order to get an inkling of the very complex web of karmic linkages, let us imagine the total current karmic force of one person as a huge vibrating cable. The cable is made up of innumerable strands. The cable ends in the present moment but its continuity goes back in time to previous lifetimes through many divergent strand connections that are all vibrating. Some strands stop in certain lifetimes. Some go back many, many lifetimes. Each strand has continuity backward only through other strands, and not as one stand-alone strand going all the way back.

Now, let us consider one factor out of the many that

cause the woman to fall in love with the man; let's say she is
captivated by the way the man pronounces certain words.
That captivation is analogous to the vibration of one strand
at the present moment. The vibration of this particular
strand is due to the vibration of previous strands. The
woman, an ardent lover of music from childhood, is en-
thralled by a unique tinge in the man's pronunciation because of a certain sound she heard in a moment of ecstasy at
a concert in Australia years before. So her response to the
concert caused her to be captivated by the man's pronunciation. She attended the concert in Australia because of three
prior causes (three strands): one, her interest in corals attracted her to Australia; two, she had worked overtime and
collected money for the trip; and three, a month earlier, she
had decided to cancel a vacation to Mt. Kilimanjaro, in
Tanzania, because she was too depressed. The depressed
mood that deterred her from going on a Tanzanian vacation
was the result of seven preceding causes, and so on and so
on. In this way, the cause-and-effect web works backward
endlessly through this lifetime and previous lives, like the
branches of a never-ending tree.

We have simply traced back from just one strand of
that relationship. When we consider the other strands of this
unique event and continue to work backward, we realize
that an unfathomable cause-and-effect structure exists link-
ing the present event to the endless past. Thus, everything
that happens to us every moment of our lives is determined
by complex cause-and-effect chains from the past. However,
we do not have to allow ourselves to be shaken by the
vibrations of the prior strands if we choose not to, because

the ability to either cut the strands or tie in new strands is in our hands at the present moment. In spite of the complex web of past karma, the future direction of our existence is in our control if we choose to exercise it. This is the supreme factor that makes humans different from all other forms of life.

When it comes to people, especially friends and family members, there are very strong reasons why they are with you and have become part of your life. Some of them will bring you comfort and happiness, and others will bring you pain and discomfort. Whatever differences, disagreements, weaknesses, or strengths there are between you, you should not purposely hurt anyone for any reason. In a karmic sense, you are attracted to each other for known or unknown reasons. Ultimately, the purpose should be creating and sharing peace, harmony, and love.

CHAPTER EIGHT

The Mind-Body Connection

The whole of the universe, oh monks,
Lies in this fathom-long body and mind.

THE BUDDHA

✤ASK YOURSELF✤

The body is a physical object; the mind is not. Together they make you who you are. Have you ever taken time to explore the relationship between the body and the mind?

Reflect for a moment on your personal experience of how the body affects the mind, and how the mind affects the body. Do you believe in the mind's ability to make your body sick or to heal it?

Your health is extremely important to living a happy life and fully enjoying its blessings. Hence the saying "If you lose health, you lose everything." Health should always be one's highest priority. To maintain or restore good health, you need to achieve balance in body and mind.

What does it mean for you to be healthy? What is your personal action list for maintaining good physical health? And what about your mental health? Do you notice unhealthy thoughts, feelings, or emotions growing in your mind? Did you know that unhealthy mental states can affect your immune and nervous systems? How often do you notice unhealthy mental states causing you pain or suffering? What would you do to keep your mind healthy? What does it mean for you to be mentally healthy?

MIND TO BODY

We all have had experiences of how the mind influences the body for better or worse. When I think about how the mind affects the body, one unforgettable event stands out in my memory.

When I was a young novice monk, I participated in a ceremony with my teacher and older monks. Unexpectedly, I was asked to speak to the gathering. The request came from an elderly lay participant who knew me well.

The request took me by surprise. I was shy and frightened to speak in front of my teacher and senior monks. I had never spoken in front of them before. I felt as if I had been asked to walk on water, and I imagined that I would sink while everybody watched. The moment I was asked to speak, my mouth became dry. I began to sweat and almost fainted. I thought of one thing and spoke of something else. Nothing made sense; everyone looked strange to me. I was afraid to look at my teacher's face. When I reflect back on that event now, I can imagine the big smile that he might have had. I talked for about five minutes. It seemed like the longest five minutes of my life.

Although no one did anything to me physically, I felt as though someone had beaten me up. My body was crippled by my mind. I still remember the incident and many others that taught me firsthand the effect of the mind on the body. Now, when I hear stories of a man fainting upon seeing an intruder in his house, or a father who had never swum before rescuing his drowning child, or an elderly grand-mother of ninety pounds lifting a full-size car to save her grandson from being crushed, I can believe them all.

Psychologists attribute these phenomena to the "fight-or-flight response," first identified by Dr. Walter Cannon at the Harvard Medical School. This is a mechanism that we have inherited from our ancestors of long ago. When confronted with a dangerous situation—for example, a ferocious wild animal preparing to attack—this physiological mechanism kicked in to help our ancestor either fight the animal or flee toward safety.

Our ancestors required the fight-or-flight response to meet the situations in their hostile environment, where the potential for physical danger lurked everywhere. But now such physical danger is the rare exception rather than the order of the day. Unfortunately, our evolutionary intelligence did not get the message that the fight-or-flight response is rarely needed in today's world. So we still carry the same mechanism as our ancestors did, and it gets activated exactly as it did during their time—only now more from our thinking than from actual physical threats. Our autonomic nervous system, which is responsible for the fight-or-flight response, does not know the difference between a genuine physical threat and an imagined threat, and therefore it responds to both in the same manner.

Just like mechanical systems, all this overload on our bodies causes them to break down. If you operate your washing machine at home twenty-four hours a day every day, it probably will not last a year, because it was designed to be used two or three times a week and to last for twenty years. The same principle applies to our bodies.

So what is the solution? Obviously, we need to ensure that our fight-or-flight mechanism is not made to work on more than it is designed to handle. We can achieve that by teaching our mind to refrain from sending recurrent false alarm signals to activate the fight-or-flight response. That can be accomplished through various stress management techniques such as visualization, cognitive therapy, and, best of all, meditation.

A Spiritual Attitude to the Mind and Body

In order to truly appreciate the importance of providing help to the mind and body, let's look at the partnership from a spiritual standpoint.

When we gaze at the sky on a clear night, we see a universe made up of celestial bodies such as stars, galaxies, and planets. Our very existence depends on one star, the sun. It supports us faithfully, rising every morning, setting every evening, providing us with the energy we need to live. The moon gives us soothing moonlit nights and regulates the oceans' tides. Venus guides home sailors who are lost at sea. Those are just a few of the myriad forces and activities out there in the great, mysterious universe. What we see appears solid and still to the naked eye, but there is really incessant movement and change.

Twenty-five hundred years ago, the Buddha spoke of the human microcosm, the universe within. He spoke of the systems within us that are invisible to the eye. These are always in motion even though the outside body appears solid and still. The Buddha tried to show us that the universe within is subject to the same laws as the outer universe.

Both universes are something to marvel at. But do we really marvel at the magic of the universe within us as much as we do at the universe without? Many of us take our bodies and minds for granted. Instead of marveling at them, we abuse them. We abuse the mind with emotions such as hatred, fear, lust, and jealousy. We neglect our bodies by not feeding or exercising them properly or by poisoning them with alcohol and nicotine.

To change our attitude toward our mind and body, first ponder how the miracle of life begins with the union of two minuscule cells, the sperm and the ovum. Then the fetus begins to grow with amazing complexity and at great speed, developing organs and systems that surpass those of all other life forms, anything that humans can create, and all other phenomena of the physical universe.

A change of attitude also requires an ability to "see" what is going on in the human being beneath the superficiality of our outer physical form: a heart that beats a lifetime; a mind that is active twenty-four hours a day; a defense mechanism—the immune system—that makes the U.S. defense system look like child's play; billions of cells working harmoniously together.

Understanding this miraculous inner universe should be enough to convince anyone of the need for a complete and permanent change of attitude toward our mind-body partnership. We need to shift our attitude away from neglect and indifference and toward care, love, and reverence. That is the spiritual attitude I am speaking of. If we don't develop that attitude, we will have to face the consequences.

HURTING THE BODY
AND MIND

One way that we hurt our body and mind is by abusing alcohol, smoking, and using illegal drugs. These substances lead to addictions that compound any problems the user has to face. A genuine spiritual seeker gives up these habits before he or she treads too far down the path, because their ill effects become barriers to progress. Giving them up becomes a test of one's spirituality. The first step in giving up the habits is to understand how harmful these substances are.

A man who is a heavy smoker once became angry with me when I mentioned that spirituality and smoking do not mix. He asked, "Bhante Wimala, what does my smoking have to do with my spirituality? I am a very spiritual person, and I know many other smokers who are spiritual." I told him that it all depends on how he defines spirituality. Let me explain.

A basic premise of spirituality is not to harm oneself or another intentionally through one's actions, words, or thoughts. The reason for saying that smoking, drinking alcohol, and partaking of illegal drugs are not characteristics of a truly spiritual person is that anyone who harms the body with negligent behavior can be considered lacking in true spiritual awareness and strength.

Breaking long-established addictions is difficult and can be painful. However, as we discussed, by developing an awareness of our inner universe and a willingness to work at eradicating these habits with diligence and patience, it is certainly possible to break away from them. Specifically, try meditating on the breath every time the urge for addictive behavior appears, or cultivate mindfulness to understand the addictive behavior of the body and mind. Those actions will help to divert attention from the addiction and will also bring numerous other spiritual benefits. Think of the rewards you will reap from the hard work: a sense of self-worth, self-control, well-being, and peace. Isn't all that worth a month or two of painstaking effort?

On Drugs and Spirituality

In my spiritual work, I try to associate with people from all walks of life. The spectrum ranges from very healthy and health-conscious people to severe drug addicts and other substance abusers. Among them, unfortunately, are even some who have pushed themselves to the point of no return mentally and who probably will remain out of touch with reality for the rest of their lives. I believe that I would fail in my spiritual mission if I favored the healthy and ignored those who are not. In fact, the people who need spiritual help the most are the ones with problems, whatever those problems may be.

Drug users take these substances for one reason—to "feel great." Other terms they use to describe that goal are to "get high" or to have a "psychic experience." Some of them have heard of the serious long-term effects. But they don't care about the long-term effects; they are interested only in getting high now, at whatever cost.

In spite of all the mounting scientific evidence about the destructive nature of these substances, there are many people in today's society who believe that drugs can help them to have spiritual experiences. I am acquainted with one well-known teacher who advocates using drugs to have spiritual experiences. A truly spiritual teacher would never recommend or encourage the use of drugs in any way. Some believe that casual use of drugs is harmless. They do not realize that it does not take very long for a casual user to become an abuser and then an addict. An often-quoted saying about alcohol goes something like this: "Man takes a drink, then the drink takes a drink, and finally the drink takes the man." Of course, this applies to all drugs, not just alcohol.

The emotional and physical damage caused by drugs

is not only to the user, but also to his or her family and society. The cost of drug abuse worldwide runs into billions of dollars. I make it a point to strongly advise my students, particularly teenagers and young adults, never to touch drugs and to keep their distance from where they are circulating.

It is very important to realize the difference between feelings of elation caused by drugs and those achieved through spiritual development. Drugs can provide only short-lived hallucinogenic experiences, and their intake causes damage, sometimes permanent, to the body and mind. Spiritual development brings peace and does not cause any damage to the body and mind; in fact, it promotes one's overall well-being. That is the reason why the Buddha and his respected disciples advocated complete abstinence from any intoxicating and stimulating drugs, including alcohol. In the Five Precepts that every true Buddhist is expected to follow, the fifth is abstinence from intoxicating drinks and drugs.

Is the reward of a few transient hallucinogenic visions or feelings worth all the pain, suffering, sickness, and death caused by these drugs? The evidence is so overwhelming that no one with any sense of the value of human life would ever touch drugs. If you already use unhealthy drugs, summon all the spiritual strength you can to give them up and move toward genuine spiritual happiness through drug-free means, namely, genuine meditation.

KAYANUPASSANA

Recognizing the effect on the body of unhealthy states of mind, Buddhism has included in its practice a body-awareness meditation called *kayanupassana*. The purpose of *kayanupassana* is to train the mind to get in touch with the emotions through the body while one is doing breathing meditation. For example, when an uncomfortable sensation rises in the body, it is due to the mind's reacting emotionally to something causing tension in the body. One could easily get lost in the emotions if this is not observed. Emotional disturbance prevents calmness of mind and relaxation of the body. *Kayanupassana* helps one to become aware of the body, relax the body, and then let go of the emotions. Once you are free from the discomfort of the physical sensation, you can get back to the focus on the breath. This meditation trains one to see the state of one's body in relation to emotions. The technique helps the emotional forces to achieve a balance, and it facilitates the natural flow of body energy.

The key to body-awareness meditation is to relax muscular tension. Modern-day stress management provides for this through various relaxation techniques, such as progressive muscle relaxation, that do not require any special equipment. In contrast, biofeedback uses a machine to measure muscular tension, blood pressure, and body temperature; the readings are displayed to the patient, who can learn to lower them by consciously relaxing.

As we have already seen, persistent emotional stress causes corresponding tensions in the body. There are specific muscular tensions associated with emotions such as anger, fear, hate, and sadness. While removing the underlying causes will be the permanent solution to these emotional disturbances, temporary relief of the tensions can be achieved by relaxing the affected muscles. The following exercise can be carried out as part of an integrated relaxation program or as preparatory to an actual meditation.

BODY RELAXATION

This exercise will help you to listen to your body and be more aware of physical sensations. We will mindfully relax the body, paying attention to one area at a time.

Sit comfortably or lie down. Close your eyes. For a minute or so, be aware of your whole body and generally observe its movements and sensations.

Now we will systematically scan and become aware of all parts of the body. Start by paying attention to the top of your head. Feel the subtle sensations in that area. Now, think the word *relax* and let the top of your head be relaxed. Then feel the forehead. Notice if there is any pressure or tension in that area. Again, think the word *relax* and try to experience relaxation in the forehead.

Next, move your awareness to your face. Notice whatever sensations you can feel on the face. Let the cheeks, eyebrows, and lips all become relaxed.

Now relax your neck and shoulders. Make sure your shoulders are loose and comfortable.

Continue the awareness and relaxation of your arms, chest, and abdomen. Watch the rise and fall of your abdomen as you breathe in and out. See whether you can feel any predominant sensations in that area. Continue to think the word *relax* and use your mental energy to encourage your muscles to relax.

Next, relax your back, buttocks, thighs, calves, and feet. Take time with each area to feel and notice the sensations and to consciously relax. Notice any predominant sensations of tension, tightness, pain, or unusual discomfort. Thinking the word *relax,* direct your mind to each area and fully relax it.

If necessary, try this relaxation exercise several times to achieve a complete state of physical relaxation. When the body is relaxed, you will notice how the mind automatically begins to slow down. Practice being mindful of your breathing for a few minutes before stopping.

This brings us to the end of this relaxation exercise.

THE TEMPORARY SHELTER

Sometimes it is useful to leave aside the abstract aspects of Buddhist philosophy for a moment and look upon the body as a temporary shelter that the individual consciousness has inherited. We Buddhists believe that our existence through innumerable lives is a very long journey indeed, and we are in this body, in this present life, only for a very short time. Even if you live to be a hundred years old, measured against that long journey of *samsara*, which is the cycle of birth and death, life is like a dewdrop at the tip of a blade of grass that soon disappears with the rising of the sun.

Because of the uncertainty of life, any day at any time we could drop this body and continue to move on in the long journey of *samsara*. But as long as we inhabit this body, it is the instrument through which our consciousness expresses itself—all the more reason to understand, be aware of, and be in touch with the forces of the body.

Although the body is a temporary shelter, it is your home in this lifetime and is deserving of care. After death, the body will decompose and revert to its permanent owner—nature. To think of the body in this way is to realize the futility and transitory nature of all attachments and the urgency of developing ourselves spiritually, for it is only spiritual development that we can carry over into our next life in our journey through *samsara*.

MIND OVER BODY

In recent experiments with hypnotism, psychologists have discovered what incredible tasks can be performed under hypnotic trance. When a person is hypnotized, the body accepts as true whatever the mind holds as truth. I have witnessed a woman under a hypnotic trance heal a rash that for years she had been unable to cure by any other means.

When I was a young monk, my teacher sent me to a small temple to be the resident monk. Except for the teenage boy who took care of the temple, most of the time I lived there alone. The temple was located in Sri Lanka's ancient city of Anuradhapura and was surrounded by ruins.

My enthusiasm for hypnotism was triggered when I discovered that a man who lived across from the temple knew how to hypnotize. We teamed up and tried different hypnotic experiments on local volunteer boys, including the caretaker of the temple. Of course, we had to do this experimenting in secrecy because my teacher would not have approved of my becoming involved with such activities.

One of the most striking observations we made with hypnotism was understanding the power of the mind over the body. The boy caretaker was the most cooperative of our subjects. Once when he was in a hypnotic trance, we gave him a glass of unsweetened lemon juice, told him it was sweet orange juice, and asked him to drink it. To our surprise, as he drank the sour liquid he made the usual facial expressions that one would make when drinking something sweet and delicious. Obviously, what his mind believed, his body felt, regardless of the reality.

We became even more interested in exploring the mind's influence on the body. The next time, after getting the caretaker into a hypnotic trance, we heated the handle of a spoon and told him that it was a very cold and soft object and that it would be soothing if he touched it. The first time we did this, I was concerned that the experiment might hurt the boy, but my hypnotism guru assured me that it would not. In fact, he said that not feeling pain was one of the objectives of hypnotism.

So, after suggesting to the boy several times that the

handle of the spoon was cold and soothing, he touched it with his fingers and held it for a while. Again I was surprised at the boy's reaction. He told us the spoon felt cold and soothing. And, amazingly, there were no red burn marks on his fingers.

I was thrilled with the results and told my guru that I wanted to continue experimenting. The next time, we tried the reverse of the previous exercise. We took a pencil and suggested to the boy that it was a hot object. We warned him to be careful. As we touched his fingertip with the pencil, he would pull away his hand as though it were, in fact, a hot object. I was greatly surprised when I examined his finger and found that there was a red mark this time.

I wondered how, without any heat or fire, it was possible for a cold pencil to burn a finger. Again, it was not the reality that was important, but what the mind *thought* the reality was. I wondered how much of what we perceive as real through sensory observation is, in fact, truly real.

The power that the mind has over the body is staggering. Using that power to our advantage, we can work toward perfect health. Many health care practitioners have said that most of our trips to doctors are due to problems that are psychological or psychosomatic rather than physiological. Therefore, it follows that if we direct our powerful mental energies toward wellness, our trips to physicians will be drastically reduced. The doctors may have to find other means to supplement their income, but what a happy problem.

BUDDHISM AND SEX

First let us try to understand some basic facts about sexuality. Nature's intent for sexuality is biological—the propagation of the species—and that is why the sexual impulse is so strong. Sexuality does not end with satisfying an urge, though modern society has created an irrational and artificial emphasis on the satisfaction of this urge. Rather, sexuality goes far beyond that to many other possibilities, including procreation and the resulting complex and enormous responsibilities.

Second, the triggers work through the sensory "doors" causing desire, just as desire is caused for anything else—for example, one's desire to eat chocolates when one sees them displayed in a store.

Third, the manifestation of the desire is psychophysiological, that is, it involves mental and bodily changes that include psychological arousal and hormonal action.

Buddhism, like many other religions, recognizes that sexuality can become a hindrance to spiritual development because of the problems mentioned above. Buddhism respects the freedom of choice of those who choose the propagation of the species as a priority over spiritual development or vice versa. These individuals comprise the Buddhist laity, some of whom may devote the major part of their time to worldly activities while others devote most of their time to spiritual development.

Buddhism recognizes the need for sexual fulfillment for the laity so long as it does not in any way cause harm to oneself or others. Hence the reference in Buddhism to "refraining from sexual misconduct" instead of "sexual abstinence." Sexual misconduct is the cause of much personal and social turmoil. The Buddha recognized that of all the sensual desires, the most difficult to control is sexual desire. Therefore, the Buddha advised all lay people to have loving, respectful, and committed relationships with their sexual partners, a relationship that society labels as marriage.

Those who have chosen to dedicate their lives fully toward their spiritual development do not obviously carry the responsibilities and complexities that follow sexual involvement. In Buddhism, these are the monks and nuns. Because sexuality can become a major hindrance to their spiritual progress, they are required to take a vow of celibacy. It should be noted that their commitment is to give up *all* sensual pleasures, and sexual pleasure happens to be only one of them. Monks and nuns, as dedicated truth seekers, work toward a higher level of spiritual happiness by sacrificing transient sensory gratification, including sex.

Until they achieve a heightened level of self-awareness and spiritual development, monks and nuns are not free from the influence of biological and emotional forces. Some people believe that as soon as somebody becomes a monk or a nun this biological need automatically disappears, and they expect them not to have any sexual attractions. That is unrealistic. Biological urges that have evolved through millions of years cannot be overcome merely through denial or repression, or by cultural and religious restrictions. They can be overcome only through proper mental training, as is taught and done in Buddhism to bring about control over all forms of sensory gratification. For dedicated truth seekers, the renunciation of all sensory pleasures means that all energy can be directed toward realizing the true happiness and purity and tranquility of mind achievable through inner transformation.

The Mystery and
Magic of the Mind

On clear, starry nights, I go outside and gaze at the sky. I am always amazed at the vastness of the universe: thousands of stars visible to the naked eye, millions upon millions beyond the limits of our vision, and a sky whose extent is unknown. Along with feelings of enthusiasm and excitement, I am filled with wonder and reverence because this fascinating, beautiful universe is, at the same time, a great unfathomable mystery.

When I walk back home and settle down for my last meditation session of the day, I close my eyes and slowly bring my mental chatter under control. As I look deep into my mind I experience another universe, an inner universe extending into eternity. Like the outer universe, it is a mysterious and magical place. It has boundless energy and creativity, manifesting in the unique entity I think of as *myself*.

To observe the outer universe, I step into an open field. To observe the inner universe, I step into a quiet place within myself. From that quiet place, I observe the busy and noisy activities of my mind. At times I am startled by its speed. The memories, imaginations, fantasies, and thoughts all compete among themselves to take center stage.

I think all the time. Even when I am sleeping, my mind is either dreaming or acting as a "security guard," waiting to wake me if necessary. Yet this very mind that I think with all the time remains a great mystery to me.

A teacher of mine used to say that there is a saint and a criminal within each person. For some, the mind is a sanctuary; for others, it is a dark and painful prison. Both are potential states of mind driven by many forces that are hard to understand. Forming our thoughts and molding our personalities, the mind dominates our lives.

UNSEEN FORCES

The great enigma for psychologists and philosophers is the mind. Mystics have tried to understand it by treading paths of renunciation, isolation, and contemplation. As ordinary people, we may not know a great deal about the mind because we have not made it our sole topic of study. Yet we are very much aware of its power to cause suffering sometimes and to bring us happiness at other times. Our inability to get behind the mind, take the controls, and steer it in the direction we want sometimes leaves us frustrated, helpless, and confused.

Mind is seen in Buddhism as an activity rather than as an entity. Buddhists use certain terms in reference to the mind: *citta, mano,* and *vinnana.*

Citta refers to the affective or emotional part of the activity. It is usually associated with the heart, the blood, and body chemistry.

Mano refers to the intellectual or conceptual part of the activity, which is usually associated with the head or brain.

Vinnana refers to the perceptual or cognitive part of activity, which is associated with the five senses: sight, hearing, smell, taste, and touch.

Mano vinnana is a term used to describe the mental activity that processes the data collected through the five senses and constructs meaning out of them.

The mind is an activity that influences the physical behavior of all living beings. Although this mental activity is associated with every cell in the human body, its controlling center is the brain. The activities of the brain are manifested as the mind and are described with nonphysical terms such as *thoughts, emotions, will,* and *imagination.*

Think of the lamp on your table or at your bedside that you switch on to read this book. The power behind the visible light is invisible electricity. As we know, not only does electricity light the lamp, but also its power can be used to do innumerable things, such as run the TV, heat food, and move the escalators in a mall. We can see, hear, or feel its countless manifestations, but we cannot see the electric current itself.

Our mind is similar to an electric current. We can sense its manifestations as thoughts, feelings, dreams, and so on, but we cannot see the mind as a physical entity. What we think and feel consciously represents only a small fraction of the mind. Some might perceive the mind as the processing center for sensory information, and thoughts and feelings as the results of that processing. Yet the mind extends far beyond thoughts and feelings.

This enigmatic, elusive, yet powerful force of the mind seems to know no limits. It can direct the body to relax at the beach or help find ways to travel to the moon and return to earth safely. It can cause one to help needy children or become a serial killer. Whatever its power, mystery, and magic may be, this force is our constant companion night and day.

THE POWER OF FAITH

Faith is believing in something without proof, or before anticipated results are delivered. Sometimes we see results, but often we end up frustrated. Think of some acts of faith in your own life, whether the anticipated results were delivered or not. Perhaps you had faith in a religious leader. You may have made some offerings at a shrine so that a wish could be granted. Maybe you prayed to a divine person to relieve you from suffering or to help you with a special problem. Have your experiences with faith made you a strong believer? Or have they made you a convinced nonbeliever? Do you know anyone else for whom faith has made an impact one way or the other?

In theological terms, faith is the acceptance and trust in the will of God, the Creator. It is not within the scope of this book to discuss the validity or invalidity of theological faith. However, what I have found to be interesting and useful is the psychological effect of having faith in anything, be it a god, idea, person, or object. When one has unshakable faith in something, it can unleash extraordinary powers of the mind that, in turn, can help bring about the desire or wish.

The power of faith is not exclusively religious. It can be a strong trust in anyone or anything, and it is a uniquely personal experience. Most of all, have faith in yourself, have faith that your spiritual potential can liberate you, and have faith in goodness, happiness, peace, and love. Real faith will always be faithful to you.

AFFIRMATIONS

Affirmations are highly effective mind-training tools that can help one to progress toward spiritual goals by consciously reinforcing wholesome thoughts relevant to those goals.

Affirmations take one much further than mere thinking or wishing. Through repeated practice, they enable one to be what the words of the affirmations intend. In fact, one meaning of the word *affirm* is "to maintain something to be true." Thus, if a person who is presently inclined toward hatred can bring himself or herself to repeatedly say "I am loving" day after day, the mind will soon cause his or her actions to be tinged with love—though, in the beginning, the wholesome virtue may appear only to a small degree. If the person is already in a loving disposition, the practice of that affirmation will strengthen his or her disposition and develop it to an even higher level.

What is true of positive affirmations is, of course, equally true of negative affirmations. A common negative affirmation is "I can't do that," which often is a fully matured carry-over from what was initially said by someone who had a significant influence in one's early life, such as a parent, teacher, or older relative. People often carry the effects of such affirmations right through adulthood into old age (and pay a heavy price for it) unless steps are taken to correct them. One obvious way to do that is to become aware of the negative belief and use a superimposing positive affirmation.

Affirmations work because the autonomic nervous system cannot differentiate between real and imaginary input. By repeating affirmations, we are overriding an unwholesome thought with a wholesome one. The more an affirmation is repeated, the more it becomes ingrained in the mind and, therefore, begins to condition one's behavior. In other words, the thought or the view one reflects upon becomes part of one's conditioning, and that conditioning influences one's behavior.

I use an affirmation containing three important words every day after my meditation: "I am kind, loving, and patient." The practice (not only of this affirmation, but of any affirmation) always has the potential to go beyond mere words. Having mentally uttered the words, I spend a few minutes contemplating what I mean by them, thereby helping along the process of new and wholesome mental conditioning.

Here are some guidelines for practicing affirmations, using the example of my favorite affirmation, "I am kind, loving, and patient."

- Clearly know and remind yourself that you want to be kind, loving, and patient.

- To nurture lovingness in yourself, free yourself from judgments based on negative beliefs about who you are. For example, if you believe that you have been an unkind, unloving, impatient person in the past, it does not mean that you are doomed to be so forever. In reality, there are no unkind, unloving, or impatient *persons* in this universe, only unkind, unloving, and impatient *behaviors*. Behaviors can always be changed.

- Believe in your ability to let go of what is not loving within you.

- When practicing the affirmation, try to focus on the meaning of the words that you repeat in your mind.

- Continue to practice diligently until you see results. Normally affirmations take a while to work, because it takes time for the mind to get charged with the energy of your positive thoughts. If you want your affirmation to become a reality, you need to work at it consistently and patiently to achieve the results you desire.

Say the words "I am kind, loving, and patient" to yourself at specially chosen times, particularly when you catch yourself in behavior opposite to the affirmation. Reflect on the meaning of the words. If you like, you could write down the words and place the affirmation somewhere visible, such as on your desk or by your bedside.

During the initial stages of your practice, watch for resistance from the old conditioning in the form of "No, I am *not* kind, loving, and patient." This simply confirms the strong roots the old conditioning has, and is to be expected. It is effectively saying, "Yes, I know you have decided to evict me. But you just watch it!" Continue to persist with determination and remain confident that, given regular practice, time, and patience, you will eventually emerge with a new, wholesome attitude or behavior.

CHAPTER NINE

Our Planet,
Our Home

Suddenly from behind the rim of the moon,
in long, slow-motion moments of immense majesty,
there emerges a sparkling blue and white jewel,
a light, delicate sky-blue sphere
laced with slowly swirling veils of white,
rising gradually like a small pearl
in a thick sea of black mystery.
It takes more than a moment
to fully realize this is Earth
. . . home.

EDGAR MITCHELL

⤙ASK YOURSELF⤚

*L*et us venture out for a moment from whatever place we call
home to our larger home—the earth. When we were born into this
world, each one of us selected this planet as our temporary home.
We are allowed a maximum stay of about one hundred years.

Reflecting back on your sojourn here thus far, have you ever thought of yourself as a citizen of the world rather than one country? Can you step beyond man-made boundaries and think of this earth as one country, one nation? Visualize extending yourself beyond you, your family, your nationality, your race, and so forth, and see yourself as a member of one large family—the human family, with no such boundaries. How would you describe your relationship with fellow human beings, the members of your family? How would you want the other members of the family to treat you?

Nature treats all human beings alike, eschewing social boundaries, labels, and prejudices. We were born empty-handed, and we will die empty-handed. We all breathe the same air and are nourished by the same natural resources; the sun and the moon shine equally on us all. Just as you care for your apartment or home, have you ever thought about your responsibility to care for, protect, and support the good health and well-being of the earth, our real home?

TRIBAL FAMILY

Sri Lanka is my birthplace, and it is where my relatives live. In that sense, it is my home country. When I left Sri Lanka and began to travel, my sense of home and family changed dramatically. My home expanded from the smaller unit called a country to the bigger one called the world. During the past fifteen years, the entire world has been my home. I have traveled to and lived in many countries. I have intimately experienced the diversity and beauty of the human community. People from around the world now constitute my extended family. This embracing of a larger home and family has been an amazingly fulfilling and nurturing experience for me; it has expanded my heart.

People frequently ask me, "Bhante, how often do you go home? Don't you feel homesick?" Yes, when I left Sri Lanka for the first time I did feel homesick. However, it didn't take too long for me to discover a much larger home and family. Beyond Sri Lanka and my biological family, I discovered the human family in the home of planet Earth.

There have been many occasions when I've deeply experienced this feeling of family and home in different places around the world. Let me share one such special moment with you.

Many years ago during my travels in Nepal, I went to the mountains to meditate for a few days by myself. I stayed in a small hut at the foot of the mountains. The hut belonged to a person I had befriended in Katmandu. One afternoon I went for a stroll in the mountains, and it became dark before I could return to the hut. While looking for a place to stay the night, I wandered into the home of a tribal family—a mother, father, and two children.

Obviously, I didn't speak their language and they didn't speak mine. So, before long, we began to speak with signs and gestures. After only a few exchanges in sign language, it became clear to me that my hosts understood that I was lost in the mountains and was looking for a place to stay the night.

They were warm, friendly, and kind people. They lived in a single-room hut with a bed suspended from the ceiling. While the father and mother cooked dinner, I played with the children. The only source of light was a single oil-burning lamp hung on the wall, which had turned brown from the smoke of the adjacent woodstove. When it got cold, we sat around the fire used to cook the dinner. The cooking pot was balanced on three rocks, and the firewood was placed under the pot. All the food was mixed and cooked together.

By now I had gotten over the initial discomfort I had had with the hut's unpleasant smell and its lack of cleanliness. Obviously, these tribal people were not bothered by the dirt, mud, and dust in the hut because they were used to this way of life. I was beginning to feel more comfortable and more at home as each minute passed.

Soon it was dinnertime, and the woman served the food on clay dishes. I discovered that the meal contained meat, so I politely refused to eat. They were disappointed but seemed to understand that the refusal was because I am a vegetarian. There was no other food in the hut that they could offer me. At that time, having a place to sleep was more important for me than food, so I was content with a cup of tea.

Later, the others joined me in sipping tea. There were smiles and nods, with occasional laughs, as we drank the steaming tea. At times, when we were trying to communicate something in gestures, it became very funny and we all laughed. The children had the most fun. Just then I suddenly felt a warmth in my heart that turned into bliss. It was a moment of heightened awareness, and in that hut in the mountains of Nepal, far away from my birthplace, I knew the world was my home.

Life has a special poetry to it. Every encounter has the potential to unfold into a fascinating story. And so it happened in that hut—strangers from two different corners of the world unexpectedly coming together and sharing love, peace, and friendship of the human spirit.

Externally, nothing was common between us. We did not even share a language with which we could communicate. That tribal family opened their home and hearts to me, and I opened my heart to them. Suddenly all mistrust and other concerns were gone. The stories of fear about strangers in strange lands lost their meaning. It was a moment of self-discovery. I experienced a deep truth about the power of the pure human spirit.

We parted company the next day with a mutual feeling of honor and respect. I knew that I may never meet them again in this life. But that experience and the lessons I learned from it influenced forever the way I feel about this beautiful world and its people. It is my firm belief that the feeling that all of us must carry deep within us is: "Wherever I am on this planet, I am home; whoever I am with are members of my human family."

As I regularly travel around the world, I deeply experience that feeling of home everywhere. Sometimes sitting by a river or under a tree, walking on a beach or in the woods, hiking up a hill or just looking up at the clouds, the inner knowing that the planet is my home flows into my heart. Having a meal with a family that I have just come to know, I feel I am home. Speaking to a group of strangers whose eyes are meeting mine for the first time, I feel as though I am talking to members of my family. In spite of language barriers, when it becomes possible in far corners of the world to share a smile or laughter with other human beings, I know I am at home, speaking to a brother or sister with the language of the heart.

FROM HOUSE TO HOME

The quote from the astronaut Edgar Mitchell that appears at the beginning of this chapter is quite moving. Yet no words can ever fully describe the feelings that must have overtaken him when he saw Mother Earth come into view, still so far away from his ship.

We often don't fully appreciate the warmth and comfort of our homes until we are far away from them. So when Mitchell speaks of the earth as home, we can imagine the many feelings that arose in him, seeing the earth not just as a planetary mass, but as an almost mystical place to which he looked forward to returning.

For many of us, the earth is a house and not a home. We effectively mark time in it until it's time to leave. During our stay, we are unaware of how it supports our existence. We destroy it through pollution, deforestation, the annihilation of certain animal species, and so on. Our vision does not go beyond "me" and "mine," living in our own little world, oblivious to what's going on beyond. Love for others is either nonexistent or is a narrowed-down version that does not extend beyond our immediate family. But life doesn't have to be that way.

There are very few among us who will have the opportunity to view the earth from the same perspective as did Mitchell. However, we can develop the same reverence for our larger home that the astronaut experienced, without ever having to leave it. This reverence and fascination come when we extend the feelings that we have for our immediate family members to all beings. And it comes when we can feel the same warm connection to it that we feel for our own personal homes.

IN YOUR HEARTBEAT

In my travels as a teacher, I often speak to groups in diverse religious settings. These include Christian churches, Jewish synagogues, Islamic mosques, and Hindu or Buddhist temples. Some are mixed gatherings made up of people from all kinds of religious and cultural groups. Often I make it a point to begin my lectures with a message reminding my audience that we are all true equals on this planet.

I usually say, "For a moment, let's put aside our religious and other identities and personal beliefs. Let us recognize that first we are all human beings, and only next come our personal beliefs or identities. We have gathered here to share the truth and explore spiritual wisdom that will help all of us realize our common goal to find happiness and live in peace. In this moment, let us remind ourselves that we all are human beings whose hearts need to be nurtured."

In spite of all the knowledge that we have accumulated in the arts and sciences and the technological progress we have made, we have much work to do to realize that we are all members of one family. We need to expand our hearts so that we can love, care for, and show compassion to all people who inhabit this planet of ours.

Nature makes us all equal in human worth, and it is only biological or survival needs (such as the dark skin color of those whose ancestors had to cope with intense sun) that make us look different. It is ego that causes people to take these differences and label others as either superior or inferior.

We are divided by color, class, nationality, and race. We are divided by language, wealth, and religion. Nature's gift of diversity among human beings, which adds magnificent beauty to the human community, has been wrongfully used for perverted applications such as discrimination and war.

Our spiritual journey requires that we take bold and brave steps to look beyond society-defined reality and see the truth of oneness. Let us always remind ourselves that we belong to only one race, the human race. Let us step beyond the external differences and look into people's hearts and minds, to see that everyone really is the same.

Here again we can learn an important lesson from children. Human babies come to this earth having pure, unadulterated minds. Unlike adults, they do not carry judgmental attitudes, dogmas, labels, mistrust, and fears that produce discriminatory attitudes. In my travels around the world, I have held babies of all kinds—black, white, Asian.

The emotional warmth that they provide is so pure that one can only respond to them with love and care.

Observe how very young children of different backgrounds relate to one another when they are together. Because barriers such as color, nationality, race, and sex are not part of a child's world, their togetherness is one of purity. To any objective observer, the way children interact among themselves would undoubtedly be the ideal model of harmonious coexistence. Their harmony is due to accepting things as they are; in other words, they do not wish that the other person be like them.

Why can't adults live in harmony like children? As we discussed in the first chapter, it's because as we grew up we were exposed to various forms of mental pollution within the family and at different societal levels. In the process, the natural instinct to live harmoniously was replaced by various man-made prejudices based on nationality, skin color, language, and the like.

There is a wonderful lesson that we adults can learn from children: the need to shed those acquired prejudices, which are based on trivial superficialities, and begin to relate to one another as human beings with the same essence, the same inner beauty.

ON THIS BEAUTIFUL PLANET

This planet of ours is only a tiny speck in an incredibly complex, beginningless, and endless universe. Scientific studies to this date have not come up with evidence of the existence of any form of life like it. Though planet Earth is physically a speck in celestial terms, it is unique within that vast immenseness. It is unique because it is filled with beauty, wonder, magic, and, most important of all, with the miracle called human life.

But what about the planet itself? Although not alive in the same way we think of humans, animals, or plants being alive, isn't it also a form of life? Isn't this the reason we call it Mother Earth? I suggest that it is a form of life, with superior qualities of caring.

This planet did not come to occupy its unique position of supporting life in the universe easily. There needed to be a critical combination of complex factors that enabled primordial life to appear on earth. The evolution of nonhuman life—growth, decay, slow adaptation to hostile environments, change, success, failure, and continuous experimentation—took billions of years.

Then early forms of animal life appeared. The process miraculously continued until the present time. Now Mother Earth is performing a delicate balancing act with its offspring, human beings. But for how long? Carelessness on the part of either means tragedy for both. Mother Earth plays her part with grace, care, maturity, and confidence, but what about the offspring? Are human beings doing their part to ensure the delicate balance of planet and life?

The relationship of Mother Earth to the billions of individuals who occupy this planet is similar to the relationship between one human being and the billions of cells that are within. It is a case of little lives collectively making up a big life. If the cells within the body work in harmony among themselves, then the human being is at peace. If the cells go berserk, then the bigger unit, the human being, is affected. Likewise, working a step up the hierarchy, if human beings work in harmony, then Mother Earth is healthy. If we go berserk, then the planet can head toward sickness or ruination.

I believe that we are at a stage of life on this planet when many signs are appearing indicating that Mother Earth is ill. There is immense pollution on land, at sea, and in the atmosphere, largely generated by man's creation and disposal of harmful products—from aerosol cans to nuclear waste. Along with that, there is exploitation of natural resources. Through the destruction of vegetation and animal life, the critical ecosystems of the planet are being forced out of balance by human beings' selfishness and callous disregard for the continuity of life on earth. We are literally biting the hand that feeds us.

I believe there are enough resources on this planet to keep us all healthy. But it is individual greed—the I-want-to-have-it-all attitude—that is driving us to the brink of annihilation.

In order to save the planet, each one of us needs to engage in deep soul-searching and look for ways to live harmoniously with nature: to not destroy the hand that feeds us, but to nurture and care for the earth; to appreciate the position that we occupy on this planet, unique in the entire universe; to celebrate our being part of that miracle by showing through our actions that we care for not only the survival of "me" but also the survival of the bigger entity of which we are part. That new awareness, coupled with a change in our actions, is a matter of grave urgency. This may be the last opportunity we have to salvage the miracle of billions of years of painstaking evolution and keep it from disappearing forever.

The Environment and You

This we know, all things are connected like the blood that unites us. We did not weave the web of life. We are merely a strand in it.

CHIEF SEATTLE

You can't separate yourself from nature. You are nature. You can't separate yourself from the environment. You are the environment. Human beings are merely a strand in the web of life. The other important strands are animals and vegetation. If you hurt or destroy the other strands of the web, it affects the structure of the web, upon which you depend for your very existence.

When we separate ourselves from nature, in the name of progress, civilization, or economic prosperity, we alter the structure of the other strands in the web of life. The consequence? We destroy the harmony and balance of the web and, in the end, ourselves.

We need to be more aware of our dependency on the air, the sun, the earth, and the rain. We need to understand the relationship between ourselves and the plants, animals, and all other living beings. We cannot act as though we are the owners of this planet and can do with it whatever pleases our fancy. If anything, we are just visitors, like all other living beings on this planet. If we are to make meaning of our existence here, we need to know the spiritual relationship between all living things and act in harmony with that knowledge.

WHAT PRICE PROGRESS?

Progress is like a race without a finish line, a road without a destination. We are all frantically rushing, but we don't know exactly where we are heading. In the end, pursuit of progress is a meaningless mission that wastes a precious life. It is another man-made illusion built on the larger illusion of personal or group ego. It means trying to run faster than what nature has prepared us for. In the process, we often stumble, hurting ourselves, or we trample others, hurting them. Often it is a combination of the two.

Most of the harm caused by human beings to our home, planet Earth, comes camouflaged as technological progress. No one would argue that technology has given us certain conveniences and provided benefits that were not available before the advent of modern technology. However, what price are we paying for the conveniences and benefits? Do the costs justify the good things? If we look clearly at what is happening around us on the planet, the answer seems to be a definite no. Another question to ask is: Are the conveniences and benefits essential for the well-being of ourselves and others? Again, the answer seems to be a clear no.

The number-one enemy of our environment is radiation. Life can tolerate a certain amount of radiation, just as it can withstand certain levels of other hostile elements such as air pollutants. It has been able to do this over millions of years because the level of radiation has, up until the present time, come from natural sources. Now human beings have suddenly caused that balance to be upset with the introduction of more radiation, which is traceable to technology.

After radiation, the next major threat to a clean environment is acid rain. Acid rain is caused primarily by the millions of tons of sulfur dioxide poured into the atmosphere by the burning of oil, gas, and coal—all part of modern technology-based activity. Acid rain is a problem because it destroys plants and animals. Thus, important links in the ecosystem are seriously disturbed. Most of us are familiar with the contamination of vegetation and the environment through agrochemical products. Pesticides and other chemicals used in the name of agricultural efficiency and effectiveness harm all forms of life. They reach human beings directly through environmental pollution and indirectly through animal food products. Other harm caused by agrochemical products includes destruction of beneficial bacteria, contamination of drinking water, and unwitting creation of strains of pests that become more resistant to chemical pesticides.

Those and other environmental crises make a number of things apparent to us. First, our actions have brought about a state of affairs that threatens the survival of life on planet Earth. Second, the major cause of this unfortunate situation is our unrestrained push for material progress, backed by an equally unrestrained technology. Third, the root cause of it all is none other than the human ego. And fourth, urgent action is needed if we are to ensure that the earth continues on its journey through many more generations to come.

Let us recognize that there is really no need for the mad technological and industrial scramble in which we are involved. There is enough food and other essentials for all beings on earth if we decide to use these resources for the well-being of all and not to satisfy greed. Also, any technological initiative must be inspired by emulating Mother Earth's respect for nature, not designed as a target for plundering. Undoubtedly technology and industry have contributed to the well-being of people, but the amount of resources needed to obtain that benefit is a small proportion of the present enormous waste that has rebounding negative effects on all of us and our children.

OVERCOMING PREJUDICE

In the eyes of the lotus, the king and the ordinary peasant are equal. It blossoms to share its beauty free of any discrimination and prejudice. The lotus teaches us that prejudice can exist only in the heart that hasn't blossomed spiritually. As I travel to many parts of the world and meet people, I remember this important lesson. It helps me not to be prejudiced and not to allow the prejudice of other people to affect me.

There is a lot of cultural prejudice in the world, but

overcoming these prejudices has been a very satisfying process for me. Throughout history there have been rare individuals who have managed to overcome very strong cultural barriers through their clarity of vision and the sincerity of their heart. These rare, enlightened people are my inspiration as I travel. I always imagine that through their placid wisdom, they could see beyond cultural boundaries, beyond the ignorance and fear that create dogmas of aggression and isolation, and focus on the meaningful core issues of any situation.

With careful words, a gentle smile, and a heartfelt gesture, such persons are above judgment, beyond language, and perpetually welcome. When such a person makes the kind of cultural error that would be unforgivable for natives or other visitors—as I sometimes do—most people just laugh softly to themselves, blaming the rigidity of their own expectations, and consider the traveler with even greater warmth. These are universal people, and their home is with everyone.

When I meet people, I am not meeting their religious, racial, or ethnic labels; often I won't even know who they are or what they believe in. Instead, I am meeting spiritual beings with consciousness, heart, intention, and important existential information to share with me. When I travel, in my heart I see no Buddhists, Christians, Jews, Jainis, or spiritualists; no Germans, Swedes, Thais, or Israelis. I see no colors, genders, or ages. I see eager, caring, conscious people who are both struggling and playing with the same issues as everybody else. When I have that realization, I cannot help but try to extend only smiles, laughter, and understanding to all.

Of course, it is not without effort that I continue to

travel among so many different people, and not every inter-
action is as enlightened as I would hope. In Germany, I met
a fine family of Christians who pitied me since they believed
I must be lonely without God. In America, I know people
who feel that the life of a monk must be devoid of love and,
therefore, I must be suffering. I even meet Buddhists who
are not used to a traveling monk like me and who criticize
my ways. These people are sometimes quite aggressive in
the presentation of their views. And although I occasionally
feel uncomfortable, I am also interested in these views. I still
have much to learn. So I return their energy with respectful
attention. I listen to them, ask questions, exchange views,
and quietly go about my own way. It is surprising to me how
a second visit to these people often shows that they remember my respectful attention to them and not the strength of
their disapproval of me.

Our spiritual journey requires us to undertake serious
self-inquiry so that we can cleanse our hearts of the elements
of prejudice and discrimination. When your heart blossoms
like the lotus and you see the world through the eyes of such
a pure heart, you will see all human beings with respect,
caring, and love.

THE LESSONS OF
THE LOTUS

Your heart is the lotus, waiting to be awakened. As the
lotus blossoms it stays untouched by the murky water,

reminding you that if you can awaken your heart, you also will stay untouched by the ills of the world. It reminds you about the power that you have within you to overcome the imperfections of life and achieve perfection.

As it blossoms the lotus begins to make the world around it a better world. Pouring out its pure scent to the gentle breeze, it soothes the hearts of passersby. Its beauty becomes a blessing to the marsh that gave birth to it. What a wonderful way to teach us the lessons of unselfishness, unconditional love, and the virtue of giving.

When your heart blossoms with pure spiritual qualities, as did the lotus, you will be a beautiful person. You will be a likable, attractive person and will radiate the fragrance of peace. Your thoughts, words, or actions will not hurt or cause suffering to anybody in this world. Your life will be a life of service that brings peace, healing, and comfort to everybody. The lotus teaches you that by just being a pure, good, kind, and loving person, what you radiate will always be in the air around you. Then those who come to know you will easily respect you and appreciate your being.

The now blossomed lotus says, "I was once a helpless little bud struggling in the murky water in darkness. Yet throughout that long journey I carried the potential of my beauty. Look at me now. I am a symbol of beauty, peace, and perfection." Saying so, the lotus teaches you to remember that when you go through difficulties and struggles in life, or if you feel that you are worthless, you should remind yourself of your inherent beauty and divinity.

If you can become a living example of the spiritual blossoming of a human heart, think what a perfect example you will be to the world around you. Your presence will give hope and inspiration to those who struggle along their own path, just as the scent of the lotus soothed the hearts of passersby. Your peace, happiness, and love will bring healing to them. Make a firm commitment to yourself to follow the path of the lotus bud within your heart and trust the divinity within, until one day it fully blossoms.

BHANTE Y. WIMALA was born in Sri Lanka and received his ordination as a novice at the age of fourteen. He then completed seven years of formal training as a Buddhist monk and received his higher ordination at the age of twenty-one. At this stage the typical Buddhist monk is encouraged by custom or by inclination to continue in formal studies, which are primarily academic in emphasis. Bhante Wimala, however, chose a more experience-oriented path. He has traveled the planet for the past twelve years, teaching and presenting Buddhist thinking to people from all walks of life.